D1519786

COUNTRIES OF THE MIND

The Fiction of J. M. Coetzee

DICK PENNER

Contributions to the Study of World Literature,
Number 32

GREENWOOD PRESS

New York · Westport, Connecticut · London

Library of Congress Cataloging in Publication Data

Penner, Allen Richard [Dick].
    Countries of the mind.

    (Contributions to the study of world literature,
ISSN 0738-9345 ; no. 32)
    Bibliography: p.
    Includes index.
    1. Coetzee, J. M., 1940–   —Criticism and interpre-
tation.   I. Title.   II. Series.
PR9369.3.C58Z87   1989   823   88-34731
ISBN 0-313-26684-0 (alk. paper)

British Library Cataloguing in Publication Data is available.

Library of Congress Catalog Card Number: 88-34731
ISBN: 0-313-26684-0
ISSN: 0738-9345

First published in 1989

Greenwood Press, Inc.
88 Post Road West, Westport, Connecticut 06881

Printed in the United States of America

The paper used in this book complies with the
Permanent Paper Standard issued by the National
Information Standards Organization (Z39.48-1984).

10 9 8 7 6 5 4 3 2 1

FOR SUSAN

"Whereas in the kind of game that I am talking about,
you can change the rules if you are good enough.
You can change the rules for everybody if you are good
enough.
You can change the game."

John Coetzee
Writers' Workshop
Lexington, Kentucky
March 6, 1984

"Things have a life of their own," the gypsy proclaimed with
a harsh accent. "It's simply a matter of waking up their souls."

. . . .

José Arcadio Buendía ventured a murmur:
  "It's the largest diamond in the world."
  "No," the gypsy countered. "It's ice."

Gabriel García Márquez
One Hundred Years of Solitude

Contents

Preface

Since the publication of his first novel in 1974, J. M. Coetzee has attained a worldwide reputation as one of the most respected novelists
writing in English, winning ten literary awards, among them Great
Britain's Booker-McConnell Prize (1983), France's Prix Femina Etranger (1985), and the Jerusalem Prize (1987), for writing that contributes
to the freedom of the individual in society. The demand for his works
is related to the world's interest in the politics, literature, culture, and
society of South Africa. However, Coetzee's fictions maintain their significance apart from a South African context, because of their artistry
and because they transform urgent societal concerns into more enduring questions regarding colonialism and the relationships of mastery
and servitude between cultures and individuals.

Coetzee's novels both replicate and subvert traditional forms, as Jonathan Crew, Teresa Dovey, Paul Rich, and others have observed.[1] Thus,
we find in Coetzee's works transformations of the historical novel,
eighteenth-century novels of exploration and travel/adventure, the idyllic
pastoral, the liberal novel, and, as I demonstrate, the farm and agrarian-protest novel. These adaptations of earlier literary forms become
self-reflexive commentaries on the nature of fiction and fiction writing.
Coetzee's novels also employ diverse modes of discourse. For example,
Dusklands and *In the Heart of the Country* present abnormal psychological
realism; *Waiting for the Barbarians* is a realistic allegory; *Life and Times
of Michael K* combines realism and naturalism; while *Foe* has strong elements of the Absurd. Given the diversity of Coetzee's individual works,
I have considered each novel as an entity in terms of form and fictional
technique, while observing thematic unities throughout.

Despite the diversity of their novelistic forms, characterization, and
settings, Coetzee's novels all deal with what Stephen Watson has called

"the metaphysics of power," the Cartesian division between the self and others that is at the base of all colonial and master/slave thought. Many of Coetzee's protagonists who struggle to escape this Cartesian dichotomy and the colonizing mentality it fosters also hold a privileged status within their societies. Thus, they face a dilemma: even if they are personally innocent of any acts of oppression, they still share responsibility as members of the colonizing group. This paradox leads to a certain quality at the heart of Coetzee's fiction that some critics have found disturbing: a malaise, an absence, a failed dialectic. If Coetzee does not provide political solutions or a direct call to action to resolve South Africa's enormous problems, it is because he is striking at a more fundamental problem: the psychological, philosophical, and linguistic bases of the colonial dilemma.

This brings us to the question of Coetzee's identity as a South African writer, a designation he has attempted to resist. In a 1983 interview he stated: "I sometimes wonder whether it isn't simply that vast and wholly ideological superstructure constituted by publishing, reviewing and criticism that is coercing on me the fate of being a 'South African Novelist.'"[2] His concern with the label seems to have both political and cultural bases. To the media in this historical moment, to be a South African author means to be politicized and to produce works that can be adapted to political uses; Coetzee's fictions do not readily lend themselves to this. In another interview, he rejected attempts to have his novels absorbed into a South African political context, stating that "frankly, my allegiances lie with the discourse of the novels and not with the discourse of politics."[3] The consequence is that readers and critics whose interests are primarily ideological have not found Coetzee's novels very useful.

To be a South African novelist also implies a cultural context: being a part of the South African fictional tradition, which until recently has largely consisted of adapting an "existing European form to a set of new South African experiences."[4] Coetzee's tradition is broader, the Western literary tradition, of which South African letters is a part. In this book, I make connections between his works and those of authors from Europe, South Africa, the United States, and elsewhere. As Coetzee once observed, one effect of his being a South African is his awareness "that there is an enormous human variety in the world, much more than merely exists in South Africa."[5]

While Coetzee is a Western novelist, he is nonetheless a South African—in terms of his birth, citizenship, and his education at the University of Cape Town, where he received his B.A. and M.A. degrees, and where he has taught linguistics and literature since 1972. He is even more a South African by his evident love for his country's people, its languages, and landscape. In his concluding essay in *White Writing* (1988),

Coetzee observes that the artist encounters in the South African landscape an invisible and silent Sphinx which "forces upon the poet the
role of a man answering a riddle, a riddle which he must . . . pose to
and for himself. The Sphinx he confronts is in fact no different from
nothing; it is an absence. . . ." The artist has the option of meeting
the silence of the Sphinx with silence, "but what is felt with the greatest
urgency by these poets is that silence, the silence of Africa, cannot be
allowed to prevail: space presents itself, it must be filled."[6] Coetzee's
novels embody the riddles he has imagined in a landscape of silence,
and they underscore his bond with South Africa, a relationship which
must be taken into account.

The first two chapters of my book reflect Coetzee's sense of his dual
identity: as a South African citizen, and as a Western writer living in
South Africa. Chapter 1 sets forth his relation to and views of South
Africa. Chapter 2 presents two topics: first, the circumstances of writers
in South Africa; second, a description of Coetzee's five novels, followed
by a discussion of their critical reception. In the remaining chapters, I
examine Coetzee's novels and make connections between them and other
works from Western literature.

In analyzing Coetzee's fiction, I have drawn upon primary and critical texts on Western and South African literature and society, all of
Coetzee's writings (including his dissertation and over forty essays and
interviews), publications about his works (approximately fifty critical essays, not counting brief reviews), and two monographs—Teresa Dovey's study of Coetzee's works in relation to the psychoanalytic writings
of Jacques Lacan, and Jan Haluska's research on master/slave relationships in Coetzee's fiction. I have also incorporated material which I
taped when Coetzee was in Lexington, Kentucky, in March 1984: a
private interview, his lecture on Dostoevsky, remarks he made during
a two-hour writers' workshop, and his introductory statements prior to
reading from his novels. In a few instances, I have included brief ex-
cerpts from Coetzee's correspondence with me.

I do not wish for my book to appear to be anything more than what
it is, a close examination of an accomplished author's fiction. The South
Africa I know comes from books and articles, music and documentary
films, and what little the present South African government allows the
world news media to report. South Africa for me is a country of the
mind, as remotely accessible as García Márquez's Macondo and Joyce's
Dublin.

While this book reflects what I set out to accomplish, there are important aspects of Coetzee's fiction not addressed in depth here, which
await future consideration. One of the most intriguing of these topics
would be a thorough examination of the role of women characters in
his novels, a question which has not been addressed in any comprehen-

sive study. Another subject is the relation of Coetzee's works to those of Samuel Beckett, which might produce some interesting connections, since Coetzee wrote his dissertation and has published several articles on Beckett's writings. As odd as it might sound, insects have a significant place in Coetzee's novels, although I have scarcely mentioned them. Asked about the pervasiveness of these creatures in his fiction, Coetzee remarked that he finds them more interesting than animals because "insects are extraordinarily alien. . . . They seem very happy."[7] Possibly the most challenging topic would be a linguistic analysis of Coetzee's works. He is a linguist as well as a novelist, and finds teaching the science of language even more interesting than teaching literature (Sévry interview, 1). A measure of his passion for linguistics is indicated in a scenario he once imagined:

If a latter-day ark were ever commissioned to take the best that mankind had to offer and make a fresh start on the farther planets, if it ever came down to that, might we not leave Shakespeare's plays and Beethoven's quartets behind to make room for the last aboriginal speaker of Dyirbal, even though she might be a fat old woman who scratched herself and smelled bad?[8]

These and other topics await the consideration of scholars, who may be working on them right now.

I began this work, without realizing it, in the fall of 1983, when a friend gave me a copy of *Waiting for the Barbarians*. Although I had been teaching and writing about fiction, primarily twentieth-century fiction, for almost twenty years, I felt a profound admiration for that novel's resonant prose, mythic setting, empathetic characters, and most of all, for its ethical vision. I still hold it in that regard. One book has led to another. In writing this, I have learned a great deal about Coetzee's fictions, the nature of narrative, colonialism, and South Africa. It has been an enjoyable journey, one which I hope will be as beneficial to the reader as it has been for me.

Dick Penner
University of Tennessee, Knoxville

NOTES

1. Jonathan Crew, *"Dusklands," Contrast* 9, no. 11 (1974): 90–95. Teresa Dovey, *The Novels of J. M. Coetzee: Lacanian Allegories* (Johannesburg: Ad. Donker, 1988); this study is a revision of Dovey's dissertation, "The Lacanian Subject in the Novels of J. M. Coetzee," Univ. of Melbourne, 1986, with an additional chapter on *Foe*. Paul Rich, "Apartheid and the Decline of Civilization Idea: An Essay on Nadine Gordimer's *July's People* and J. M. Coetzee's *Waiting for the Barbarians*," *Research in African Literature* 15, no. 3 (1984): 365–93. See also the cited

works by Peter Knox-Shaw, Hena Maes-Jelinek, Richard G. Martin, Michael
Vaughan, and Stephen Watson.

2. J. M. Coetzee, in interview with Tony Morphet, *From South Africa*, special
issue of *TriQuarterly* (Evanston: Northwestern Univ. Press, 1987):460.

3. J. M. Coetzee, in Dovey, *Novels of J. M. Coetzee*, 55.

4. Sarah Christie, Geoffrey Hutchings, and Don Maclennan, *Perspectives on
South African Fiction* (Johannesburg: Ad. Donker, 1980), 182.

5. J. M. Coetzee, in interview with Folke Rhedin, *Kunapipi* 6, no. 1 (1984):6.

6. J. M. Coetzee, *White Writing: On the Culture of Letters in South Africa* (New
Haven and London: Yale Univ. Press, 1988), 177.

7. J. M. Coetzee, in interview with Jean Sévry, *Commonwealth* 9, no. 1 (Autumn 1986):3.

8. J. M. Coetzee, "How I Learned About America—and Africa—in Texas,"
New York Times Book Review, 9 April 1984, 9.

Acknowledgments

I wish to acknowledge my thanks to my colleagues and friends Susan Becker, Jim Gill, and Allen Dunn for their thoughtful readings of portions of the text, to Mary Francis Crawford for her valuable help in obtaining bibliographical data, to Sandra Lewis for her expert preparation of the manuscript, and to numerous others who know who they are, although their names do not appear here. I also express my appreciation to Professor Doug Killam for publishing early versions of chapters 5 and 7 in *World Literature Written in English*. I am indebted to the Graduate School and especially to the English department of the University of Tennessee for providing research time to develop and complete this book.

My thanks go to John Coetzee for granting me permission to tape-record and publish portions of an interview and the public addresses he gave in March 1984, and for providing biographical information. John Coetzee's cooperation in this matter in no way implies his authorization or approval of the views expressed in this book, for which I am solely responsible.

I also express my appreciation to Marilyn Brownstein, Patricia A. Meyers, and Maureen Melino of Greenwood Press for their very capable and professional cooperation.

COUNTRIES
OF THE MIND

Introduction

John Maxwell Coetzee has published five fictional works: *Dusklands* (1974); *In the Heart of the Country* (1977), which won South Africa's premier literary award, the CNA Prize; *Waiting for the Barbarians* (1980), chosen by the *New York Times* as one of the Best Books of 1982; *Life and Times of Michael K* (1983), recipient of two prestigious international awards, Britain's Booker-McConnell Prize (1983) and France's Prix Femina Etranger (1985); and *Foe* (1986). In addition, Coetzee has the distinction of winning the 1987 Jerusalem Prize for his "staunch opposition to apartheid and oppression in any form" and for writings which "combine extreme sensitivity to the *condition humaine* with a powerful prose condemning man's cruelty to man." Coetzee's most recent novel, *Foe*, is a retelling of *Robinson Crusoe* as well as a self-reflexive commentary on the nature of narrative.[1]

Coetzee (pronounced coot-*see*) is descended from Afrikaners who settled in South Africa in the seventeenth century. His grandparents on both sides were Afrikaner farmers. In an interview which I taped in Lexington, Kentucky, on 6 March 1984, when he was presenting a series of lectures and readings, Coetzee remarked, "Afrikanerdom is based really on comparatively few families. You find the same last names in enormous numbers all over the country. And that's an historical reflection on a small original colony that's grown by having large families. So here I am as one of a huge clan of Coetzees, who have been part of the history of that country for three hundred years." Coetzee was born on 9 February 1940, in Cape Town. His father, Zacharias Coetzee, prior to his retirement, was an attorney; his mother, Vera Wehmeyer Coetzee, was a schoolteacher; his brother is a journalist. He has two children by a former marriage, Nicolas and Gisela.

In his youth, Coetzee lived with his parents and grew up in "about twenty different places in South Africa," primarily in the vast Karoo (from the Hottentot word for "dry"), the one hundred-thousand-square-mile tableland of desert and semidesert that covers two-thirds of the Cape province. This experience laid the foundation for Coetzee's powerful descriptive passages in his novels. As Lionel Abrahams observes, "he selects the precise details necessary for his settings and makes them dense with significant associations. The primitive South African landscape in particular impinges on the inward eye."[2] Fortunate, too, for his later literary career, was his early training in English. Coetzee grew up speaking English at home, Afrikaans with other relatives. He attended various English-language schools and graduated from St. Joseph's College, Rondebosch, Cape Province, a Roman Catholic boys' school, in 1956. In addition to English and Afrikaans, he speaks Dutch fluently, and, as a linguist, is knowledgeable about a number of other languages.[3]

The facts available concerning Coetzee's adult life are primarily related to his considerable academic and literary achievements. He received his first three degrees from the University of Cape Town: B.A., honors, English, 1960; B.A., honors, Mathematics, 1961; M.A., English, 1963. Of his undergraduate experience, he later had this reflection:

In the colonies, where I came from ultimately, I had received a conventional undergraduate training in English studies. That is to say, I had learned to speak Chaucerian verse with good vowel definition and to read Elizabethan handwriting; I was acquainted with the Pearl Poet and Thomas More and John Evelyn and many other worthies; I could "do" literary criticism, though I had no clear idea of what it was, how it differed from book reviewing or polite talk about books. All in all, this patchy imitation of Oxford "English" had proved a dull mistress from whom I had been thankful to turn . . . to the embrace of mathematics.[4]

During a four-year respite from academic life, he worked as an applications programmer for International Business Machines in London, England, in 1962–63, and as a systems programmer for International Computers in Bracknell, England, during 1964–65. His experience with business made a life of letters seem a more positive embrace: "After four years in the computer industry during which even my sleeping hours had been invaded by picayune problems in logic, I was ready to have another try."

In 1965, at the age of twenty-five, Coetzee embarked from England to America, where he was to begin doctoral work in English language and literature at the University of Texas at Austin while supporting

himself teaching freshman English at a salary of $2,100 dollars an-
nually under a Fulbright exchange program. "It was never clear to me,"
Coetzee later remarked, "why the university—and the American tax-
payer—had lavished so much money on me to follow idle whims." At
the same time, he accurately predicted that the gesture was "an extraordinarily farsighted and generous scheme whose humane benefits
would be felt by all parties far into the future."

The Texas experience held mixed blessings for Coetzee. His son and
daughter were born while he was working on his doctorate. At the same
time, he felt estranged in his role as a teacher: "The students I taught
in my composition classes might as well have been Trobriand Islanders,
so inaccessible to me were their culture, their recreations, their animat-
ing ideas." Still, for one so devoted to exploring the nuances of language and literature, having access to a great library and the company
of eminent scholars afforded a wealth of discovery. Coetzee immersed
himself in Old English texts and German grammar, read Noam Chom-
sky, Jerrold Katz, and the new universal grammarians, and wrote papers on rhetorical figures in the writings of the eleventh-century English cleric Bishop Wulfstan and on the morphology of the Nama, Malay,
and Dutch languages as they had converged at the Cape of Good Hope.
In the excellent twentieth-century collection at Austin he discovered
manuscripts that Samuel Beckett had written in France while hiding
from the Germans during World War II. This eventually led to Coetzee's doctoral dissertation, "The English Fiction of Samuel Beckett: An
Essay in Stylistic Analysis," a skillfully written scholarly inquiry.

Coetzee's linguistic pursuits in Texas would lead him, ironically, to a
clearer understanding of the disparate cultures of South Africa, an
awareness that would later inform his fiction. In "books unopened since
the 1920s" he discovered reports by German explorers of South West
Africa, accounts of forays against the Nama and Herero tribes, monographs on the physical anthropology and languages of the Hottentot
and Bushman tribes, and accounts compiled by seventeenth- and eighteenth-century missionaries, seafarers, travelers, and explorers, including Coetzee's own "remote ancestor, Jacobus Coetzee, fl. 1760." This
historical figure would become the model for the rapacious, self-righteous central character in one of the two novellas comprising Coetzee's
first fictional work, *Dusklands* (1974).

Coetzee left the University of Texas, shortly before being awarded
his Ph.D., to take a position at the State University of New York at
Buffalo, where he was an assistant professor of English from 1968–71.
He later accepted a position there as a visiting professor of English,
spring, 1983–84 and fall, 1986–87. He was not fond of the harsh winter weather nor of the setting, which he described to me in a letter of
4 November 1986, as "ugly, grimy Buffalo," but he acknowledged that

he was able to get "a fair amount of work done," and indeed this must have been the case in 1968–71 when he wrote most of *Dusklands*.[5] Aside from holding a visiting appointment at Johns Hopkins University, 1986–87, Coetzee has been a full-time academic at his alma mater, the University of Cape Town, where he accepted a position as a lecturer in English in 1972. He was appointed a Life Fellow in 1983 and was promoted to professor of general literature in 1984, a position which he holds at this writing.

It is obvious that Coetzee is a dedicated scholar-teacher as well as an accomplished fictionist. He has published over forty scholarly articles and review articles in such journals as *Comparative Literature, Journal of Literary Semantics, Linguistics, New York Review of Books, Modern Language Notes,* and *PMLA.*[6] His skills as a teacher are much in evidence in his public readings and lectures as well as in writers' workshops such as the one which he conducted in Lexington, Kentucky, in 1984. When I asked Coetzee about his role as a teacher, he responded:

Am I a full time academic? Yes. I teach by preference grammar, transformational grammar. That's the kind of teaching I'm happiest with, but I can't do only that. I can't find the student numbers to justify only that. So I do teach literature as well in the English department. And I teach just all over the place, by preference. I teach Chaucer; I'm teaching a course in the eighteenth-century novel, particularly Defoe; I've been teaching a course in the literature of Africa; I'm teaching a course in contemporary American poetry, a course in the nineteenth-century American novel, and you know, just all over the place. It's basically an undergraduate institution, so one doesn't have to be a specialist, really. It has drawbacks as well, but that's one of the nice aspects.

Coetzee's devotion to teaching and to South Africa is evidenced by his maintaining his position at the University of Cape Town at a time in his life when he could probably fully support himself by writing and could most certainly obtain academic positions in less turbulent locales. As we shall see later, Coetzee's bond with the South African landscape and his reluctance to become a "writer-in-exile" also figure importantly in this equation.

NOTES

1. J. M. Coetzee's first five novels are, in order of publication, *Dusklands* (Johannesburg: Raven Press, 1974; London: Secker and Warburg, 1982; New York: Viking Penguin, 1985); *In the Heart of the Country* (London: Secker and Warburg, 1977; published under the title *From the Heart of the Country*, New York: Harper and Row, 1977; Johannesburg: Raven, 1978 [bilingual edition]); *Waiting for the Barbarians* (London: Secker and Warburg, 1980; New York: Viking Penguin, 1982); *Life and Times of Michael K* (London: Secker and Warburg,

1983; New York: Viking Penguin, 1984); *Foe* (London: Secker and Warburg, 1986; New York: Viking Penguin, 1987). Page references throughout are to either the Secker and Warburg or Viking editions, which have identical pagination. The quotation from the Jerusalem Prize awards committee is from "Coetzee Wins Writing Prize," *New York Times,* 16 December 1986, 24–25.

2. Lionel Abrahams, "Reflections in a Mirror," *Snarl* 1, no. 1 (1974):2–3.

3. *Current Biography* 48, no. 1 (January 1987): 18–21. See also the vita in Coetzee's dissertation, cited below. Stephen Watson, in letters to the author dated 21 October 1988 and 28 November 1988, has suggested that Coetzee is actually part of the white English-speaking subculture of South Africa, rather than the white Afrikaner subculture. Watson points out that Coetzee's mother is English and that English is Coetzee's first language and the primary language of his fiction. On the other hand, Coetzee clearly identifies himself as an Afrikaner and has verified the biographical information in this chapter.

4. Coetzee, "How I Learned About America—and Africa—in Texas," *New York Times Book Review,* 9 April 1984, 9. The subsequent quotations concerning Coetzee's employment and doctoral work are from this article.

5. J. M. Coetzee, in interview with Folke Rhedin, *Kunapipi* 6, no. 1 (1984): 6–9.

6. The following are J. M. Coetzee's nonfiction publications since 1969, beginning with the most recent: *White Writing: On the Culture of Letters in South Africa* (New Haven and London: Yale Univ. Press, 1988); "A Prisoner of the Thought Police," *New York Times Book Review,* 31 May 1987, 9, 46; "Apartheid: La littérature mutilée" (translation of Coetzee's Jerusalem Prize acceptance speech) *Le Nouvel Observateur* 1174 (8–14 May 1987): 57–58; "Out of Africa!," *American Film* (March 1987): 19–23; "Introduction," Marcellus Emants, *Posthumous Confession,* translated by J. M. Coetzee (1987; London: Quartet Books; Boston: Twayne, 1975); J. M. Coetzee and André Brink, eds., *A Land Apart: A South African Reader* (London and Boston: Faber and Faber, 1986); "Tales Out of School," *New Republic* 3753 (22 December 1986): 36–38; "On the Edge of Revelation," *New York Review* 18 (December 1986): 10, 12; "Farm Novel and Plaasroman in South Africa," *English in Africa* 13, no. 2 (October 1986): 1–19; "Waiting for Mandela," *New York Review of Books* 33, no. 8 (8 May 1986): 3, 6, 8; "Tales of Afrikaners," *New York Times Magazine* (9 March 1986): 19+; "The White Tribe," *Vogue* (March 1986): 490–91, 543–44; "The Taming of D. H. Lawrence," *New York Review of Books* 37, nos. 21 & 22 (16 January 1986): 33–35; "Into the Dark Chamber: The Novelist and South Africa," *New York Times Book Review,* (12 January 1986), 13, 35; "Satyagraha in Durban," *New York Review of Books* 32, no. 16 (24 October 1985): 12–13; "Lineal Consciousness in the Farm Novels of C. M. van den Heever," *Tijdschrift voor Nederlands en Afrikaans* (Cologne) September 1985: 49–74; "Confession and Double Thoughts: Tolstoy, Rousseau, Dostoevsky," *Comparative Literature* 37, no. 3 (Summer 1985): 193–232; "Anthropology and the Hottentots," *Semiotica* 54 (1985): 87–95; "Listening to Afrikaners," *New York Times Book Review,* 14 April 1985, 3, 28; "Truth in Autobiography," inaugural lecture, Univ. of Cape Town, New Series 94 (3 October 1984): 1–6; "Art and Apartheid," *New Republic* 3612 (9 April 1984): 25–28; "How I Learned About America—and Africa—in Texas," *New York Times Book Review,* 9 April 1984, 9; "A Note on Writing," in *Momentum: On Recent*

South African Writing, edited by M. J. Daymond, J. U. Jacobs, and M. Lenta (Pietermaritzburg, South Africa: Natal Univ. Press, 1984), 11–13; "The Great South African Novel," *Leadership SA* 2 (Summer 1983): 74–79; "Idleness in South Africa," *Social Dynamics* 8 (1982): 1–13; "Newton and the Ideal of a Transparent Scientific Language," *Journal of Literary Semantics* 11, no. 2 (October 1982): 3–13; "Linguistics and Literature," *An Introduction to Contemporary Literary Theory* (Johannesburg: Ad. Donker, 1982) 41:52; "Pauline Smith and the Afrikaans Language," *English in Africa,* 8, no. 1 (1981): 25–32; "Time, Tense and Aspect in Kafka's 'The Burrow,'" *MLN* 96, no. 3 (April 1981): 556–79; "The Rhetoric of the Passive in English," *Linguistics: An Interdisciplinary Journal of the Language Sciences* 18 (1980): 199–221; "Blood, Flaw, Taint, Degeneration: The Case of Sarah Gertrude Millin," *English Studies in Africa: A Journal of the Humanities* 23 (1980): 41–58; "The Agentless Sentence as Rhetorical Device," *Language and Style: An International Journal* 13, no. 1 (1980): 26–34; "Triangular Structures of Desire in Advertising," *Critical Arts* 1 (1980): 34–41; "Surreal Metaphors and Random Processes," *Journal of Literary Semantics* 8 (1979): 22–30; "The White Man's Burden," *Speak* (Cape Town) 1 (1977): 4–7; "Achterberg's 'Ballade van de gasfitter': The Mystery of I and You," *PMLA* 92 (1977): 285–96; "The First Sentence of Yvonne Burgess's *The Strike,*" *English in Africa* 3, no. 1 (1976): 47–48; "Captain America in American Mythology," *University of Cape Town Studies in English* 6 (1976): 33–39; "Nabokov's *Pale Fire* and the Primacy of Art," *University of Cape Town Studies in English* 5 (1974): 1–7; "Man's Fate in the Novels of Alex La Guma," *Studies in Black Literature* 5, no. 1 (1974): 16–23; "Samuel Beckett and the Temptations of Style," *Theoria* 41 (1973): 45–50; "Samuel Beckett's Lessness: An Exercise in Decomposition," *Computers and the Humanities* 7 (1973): 195–98; "The Manuscript Revisions of Beckett's *Watt,*" *Journal of Modern Literature* 2 (1972): 472–80; "Alex La Guma and the Responsibilities of the South African Writer," *Journal of the New African Literature and the Arts* 9/10 (1971): 5–11; "The Comedy of Point of View of Beckett's *Murphy,*" *Critique: Studies in Modern Fiction* 12, no. 2 (1970): 19–27; "Statistical Indices of 'Difficulty,'" *Language & Style* 2 (1969): 226–32; "The English Fiction of Samuel Beckett: An Essay in Stylistic Analysis," diss., University of Texas, 1969.

1

John Coetzee: South African

As previously noted, my separation of the materials in this chapter from those in the one following is a result of Coetzee's perception of the distinct roles he lives, on the one hand, as a South African citizen with views on South Africa, its history, Afrikaners, apartheid, politics, and the future; and on the other hand, as an artist, a fabulist, a conjurer of tales, one who is both an inheritor of and a contributor to the literature of the Western world.

COETZEE'S SOUTH AFRICA:
HISTORICAL PERSPECTIVE

Coetzee has expressed his views of South Africa—its people, history, politics, and racial policies—in a number of essays and interviews. To begin with, he sees the Afrikaner people, his people, as "living in a historical backwater."[1] Coetzee explained in his interview with me, "History is time on which meaning has been imposed, which we call historical meaning, so that time is not just one thing after another. It is time and event that seem to be moving in a direction." He stated that the problem with the Afrikaner concept of history has to do with "the way in which the—if you like, if one can use these words—founding fathers of the modern South African state have run the history of the country since the seventeenth century." Coetzee sees the "official" history of South Africa purveyed by the present regime as "an edifice constructed of selected fragments of the past by a historiography in the service of twentieth-century nationalist politics. It was put together for precisely the purpose of buttressing and justifying the activities of a specific political grouping."[2] Supported by this selectively distorted view of their nation's past, Afrikaners see themselves as victimized and conditioned by history, thus enabling them to "evade moral responsibility for the present and even for the future."[3] Coetzee paraphrases the typical Afrikaner rationalization: "After a century of wrong, can you be surprised that we are stubborn, unforgiving, that we cling to what we have won?" ("Listening," 28). He also quotes a fellow Afrikaner who acknowledges that their "tribe" tends to be "twenty to thirty years behind the times," particularly in regard to racial discrimination, a practice which has been steadily rejected by most of the West since the end of World War II.[4]

The problems which confront South Africa permeate its history from the earliest Dutch settlement on the Cape to the present, beginning with the colony founded by Jan Van Riebeeck in 1652, which based its economy on slave labor and through miscegenation engendered the community known today as the Cape "Coloured" people. Coetzee argues that an important historical factor contributing to the intransigence of the character of Afrikaners was the failure of the European Enlightenment to reach South Africa. While the middle class of Europe and North America were, throughout the eighteenth century, evolving "an ideology of personal freedom and the rights of the individual as against the state—the Cape Colony was asleep."[5] Afrikaners did not read Rousseau or Tom Paine, Coetzee notes, and were largely unmoved by the examples of the American War of Independence and the French Revolution. After taking over the rule of the Cape in the early nineteenth century, the British instituted the Emancipation Act of 1833, freeing slaves and giving legal rights to blacks. In response, Coetzee observes, Afrikaners, "outraged, fled the Colony in droves and moved into the unexplored interior, there 'to preserve our doctrines in purity,' as one of the pioneers put it" ("White Tribe," 544). In the Great Trek of 1835–43 Afrikaners wandered "the hinterland of Africa like the tribe of Israel in the desert," after which they spent the first half of the twentieth century struggling not to be overwhelmed by British language, wealth, and condescension. Coetzee contends that Afrikaner "history has therefore largely been a history of stubborn rejection: rejection of foreign control, of foreign ways of thinking. It is a history of holding tight to the past rather than planning toward the future. It is a history that serves the Afrikaner ill. At a time when what he needs above all is flexibility, vision, an ability to think what has not been thought before, the model that his history provides him is one of inflexibility, closed vision, a dogged reliance on old modes of thought. *It is a model that hitherto has seemed to work*" (544).

AFRIKANER TRIBALISM

At the base of the Afrikaner's problems, Coetzee believes, is the concept that "the world is *essentially* made up of tribes," a concept promoted by Afrikaner Calvinist churches, which have long held that "the division of mankind into ethnic types is a part of God's dispensation," a doctrine, Coetzee notes, which has only a meager basis in Scripture. In terms of tribal thinking, Nicolaas Diederichs, president of the Republic during the 1970s, asserted: "The individual is nothing; the individual only realizes himself in the nation." Tribal mentality provided the rationale for numerous nationalist policies after 1948: the Population Registration Act, which placed every South African in a fixed "racial category"; the Immorality Act (partially repealed, 1985) and Mixed Marriages Act (repealed, 1985), which made marriages and nonmarital unions of whites and nonwhites unlawful; the notorious resettlement "homelands policy" which forced Africans to dwell in designated, often uninhabitable areas. As Coetzee observes of Afrikaners: "The cry that man is free cuts no ice: man is born into a social order. As for freedom, the freedom of the tribe is what matters." For the tribalist, education does not exist to set the mind free; it is a "process of forming the young mind in the tribal mold" (490–91, 543–44).

Such a doctrine leads, at the very least, to what Coetzee calls "the craziness of tribalistic thinking." He cites as an example the Nationalist party's dilemma over what to do with the two and one-half million people who comprise the "Coloured," or mixed race of South Africa, who, over a period of three hundred years of interracial unions have evolved as an amalgam of Africans, Europeans, and Asians: "In one of their wilder flights, the ideologues of *apartheid* decided that although not yet a tribe, the Colored people were 'a tribe in the making,' and suggested that one day they might be removed to the arid northwest Cape Province, there to exercise tribal autonomy" (543). At its worst, the apartheid that arises from tribalistic thinking is "a doctrine and a set of social practices that scars the moral being of whites as it degrades and demeans blacks" ("Tales," 21).

In his interview with me, Coetzee addressed the illogic generated by such thinking. He spoke with restrained emotion, expressing his thoughts in a measured, deliberate manner. At one point, the confusion inherent in such racial categorizing was reflected in his own speech:

I know people in South Africa who are officially classified black, who think of themselves as white, who are white. Are they black or white? I know people who are officially classified as white, who think of themselves as African. Are they black or white? I know people who are officially classified as black . . . [corrects himself] who are officially classified as white, but that is actually a mistake in the sense that they are, in some genetic sense, black, who think of themselves as white, whose thinking is actually, perhaps, black. Are they black or white? So it seems to me the closer we come to reality, the more problematic these terms *black* and *white* become. . . . In Africa, I could look white, decide that I am black. You know, it may *be,* it may be.

In an essay on Afrikaner tribalism, Coetzee makes reference to an "academic researcher in South Africa [who] recently caused an uproar by asserting, on the basis of impeccable archival evidence, that there is barely a single Afrikaner alive who is not technically colored, i.e., does not have at least one black forebear" ("White Tribe," 543).

Genetic statistics are one thing, social perceptions are quite another, just as the "Afrikaner" in the abstract is distinct from the individuals who comprise that group. One of the criticisms that Coetzee made in his balanced, mostly positive review of Ali Mazrui's nine-hour television series, "The Africans" (1987), is that the episodes failed to convey the "African *personality*" in any intimate, individual way.[6] This individual element is very much in evidence in an essay Coetzee wrote in December 1985, shortly after he had interviewed several Afrikaners (whom he had not previously known) in the town of Stellenbosch, some forty miles from Cape Town. He found that they did not conform to the stereotype: "They do not speak contemptuously of blacks. They aren't notably intolerant in their attitudes, heartless in their conduct or indolent in their daily life. They do not seem to bear the worst marks of apartheid. . . . Their allegiances seem to lie as much with the broad South African middle class as with the Afrikaner tribe. In this respect they are typical of the generation born after 1948, a generation that . . . can afford to be more self-assured, less belligerently nationalistic than their fathers" ("Tales," 19, 21).

One representative individual whom Coetzee interviewed was Jan Boland Coetzee, a former rugby star and probably a distant relation. Jan Boland is a progressive farmer and vinter who offers incentives to his workers: competitive wages, decent housing, health care, and additional rewards for high productivity. This farmer distrusts the policies of the central government, favoring a rural order based upon small farming communities, an ideal, J. M. Coetzee suggests, which is based upon "somewhat sentimentalized memories of a feudal past" (75). Jan Boland speaks harshly of apartheid, saying that the law has created a "gulf between people. We no longer know each other. Also, we whites have simply appropriated things for ourselves, leaving the blacks and Coloureds to do the producing. It is not just. It is not a healthy state of affairs" (75). J. M. Coetzee interprets his countryman's statements in this way: to those brought up in "the twilight of a centuries-old feudal order . . . the codification of social relations into the system of racial laws known as apartheid always seemed gross and unnecessary." For Jan Boland to criticize apartheid and yet "look back nostalgically to an age when everyone knew his place, by no means proves him a hypocrite," although he probably forgets "the iron hand needed to keep the old order running" (75).

Michiel le Roux, another Afrikaner Coetzee interviewed, sees the middle-class Afrikaner as having "been absorbed into a cultural pattern that is basically American"; personal concerns are primarily for "his children, his job, his salary." In terms of national concerns, these Afrikaners have lost faith in National party policies and desire a resolution to problems at a local level at "precisely the moment in history when black South Africans are grouping together in larger and larger political blocs," rejecting local solutions to national problems. Coetzee doubts whether the "enlightened paternalism" he found in the Afrikaners of Stellenbosch can ever be joined with the "egalitarian black nationalism sweeping across the land" (75).

In a review of a book about contemporary Afrikaners, Coetzee credits the author with having detected "in the soul of white South Africa . . . the *malaise* of *waiting*" ("Listening," 3). This is borne out in the individuals Coetzee interviewed. A middle-aged woman fluctuated between two visions of the future: one in which everything was much the same, but without racial laws, another in which she and her family led a subsistence existence in a country ruled by blacks. Such ambivalence, Coetzee believes, is the consequence of long-term suppression of black dissent: "Ordinary whites now not only have no one with whom to imagine negotiating their future, but have not the vaguest idea of what blacks might be prepared to settle for" ("Tales," 21). At the other extreme, one teen-aged white man envisioned a future in which whites would "be their own masters," occupying a spacious area containing approximately three-quarters of South Africa's economic resources. Coetzee reflects: "He speaks the language, arrogantly possessive, of the enduring right-wing dream of a national homeland where the Afrikaner will be left to run his affairs without interference" (22). A more reflective response was given by a middle-aged business man, a graduate in law: "The feeling that we are directionless is widespread. People have no feeling of being on the road anywhere, or of knowing where we are on the road to" (74).

COLONIALISM

In a broader context, Coetzee sees the plight of his fellow Afrikaners and fellow Africans as the consequence of a process that began in the seventeenth century: "I still tend to see the South African situation as only one manifestation of a wider historical situation to do with colonialism, late colonialism, neo-colonialism."[7] The end result of South Africa's past is a strict social and economic dichotomy: "a group of affluent and virtually postindustrial exploiters on the one hand and on the other hand an enormous number of people who live in a world which is effectively nineteenth-century . . . a situation of naked exploitation."[8] While the Afrikaners Coetzee interviewed looked to the past with nostalgia, to the present with uncertainty, and to the future with anxiety, the nonwhite Africans with whom he has spoken hold

quite different views: "If one asks almost any African of integrity to
speak about Africa, he or she will speak about a continent abused, in-
sulted, exploited, and patronized by white foreigners, an Africa that
has not forgotten its recent history, that is still, in many ways, living in
the aftershock of colonialism, that remains angry, suspicious, determined" ("Out of Africa!" 19). Coetzee observes that the situation of
colonialism did not end when the British, French, and Portuguese with-
drew from Africa, "and it will not end when the last colony—the internal colony run by whites in South Africa—fails. In the eyes of many
thinking Africans, the economic order prevailing on the continent today is simply colonialism under another name" (19).

As for South Africa's future, Coetzee, like many Afrikaners and Africans, is pessimistic, primarily because of the intransigence of the Nationalist party: "At a time when the very foundations of its power are
tottering, the government of the Republic of South Africa refuses to
negotiate with organizations that represent post-tribal Africa" ("White
Tribe," 491). In this respect, the government, as noted earlier, seems
to be "20 to 30 years behind the times."[9] Coetzee contends that if it
had come to an understanding with the outlawed African National
Congress in the 1950s "it would have been coming to terms with a
fairly peaceable popular movement under petit-bourgeois, social dem-
ocratic leadership" ("Waiting," 3). To the contrary, the government rejected the ANC in the 1950s, charged it with being communist, and
refused to engage in a dialogue with its members. As a result, the government today "is pitted against a mass movement of far greater insur-
rectionary power than it had a quarter of a century ago, with an armed
wing far better equipped and trained, and with world opinion squarely
on its side" (3). From anyone's point of view, the prospect of détente
looks remote at this juncture.

Assuming that nonwhite South Africans do one day attain the political voice they have so long been denied, what then does the future
hold for them? For proponents of Black Consciousness, of which Ali
Mazrui is one prominent spokesperson, the Africa of the future will
emerge from the traditions of the Africa of the past which prevailed
before the onslaught of nineteenth-century colonialism; in Coetzee's
paraphrase, from "sturdy, self-reliant peasants, respected elders, tight
family ties, deeply ingrained myths and observances" ("Out of Africa!"
20). The problem with this vision, as Coetzee suggests, accurately, I
think, is that while it appropriately underscores the traditional ties that
have enabled Africans to endure incredible trials, it also romanticizes
old Africa while discounting present realities. One might say that the
proponents of traditional Afrikanerdom and of Black Consciousness
are both enticed by a Lost Past. More realistically, Coetzee projects that
the Africa of the future will have to assimilate Western technology, and

inevitably along with it, Western "rationalism, materialism, Western-style economics, the profit motive, the cult of the individual, the nuclear family, and much else un-African" (22). While Coetzee may be magnifying the future impact of the West on Africa, his vision of an Africa bereft of Western science and values conveys a chilling prospect: "Can Africa hope for anything but economic stagnation, which, coupled with a fast-rising birth rate, will mean that the future promises not a return to Eden, but a hell of disease and starvation?" (20, 22).

NOTES

1. J. M. Coetzee interview with Stephen Watson, *Speak* 1, no. 3 (1978): 21–24.

2. J. M. Coetzee, "Listening to Afrikaners," *New York Times Book Review,* 14 April 1985: 3, 28.

3. J. M. Coetzee, "Waiting for Mandela," *New York Review of Books* 33, no. 8 (8 May 1986): 3, 6, 8.

4. Michiel le Roux, quoted in J. M. Coetzee, "Tales of Afrikaners," *New York Times Magazine* 135 (9 March 1986): 19, 21, 74–75.

5. J. M. Coetzee, "The White Tribe," *Vogue* (March 1986): 489–545.

6. J. M. Coetzee, "Out of Africa!" *American Film* (March 1987): 19–23.

7. J. M. Coetzee, in interview, Watson 23.

8. J. M. Coetzee, in interview with Folke Rhedin, *Kunapipi* 6, no. 1 (1984): 8.

9. Michiel le Roux, quoted in Coetzee, "Tales of Afrikaners," 74.

2

John Coetzee: Fictionist

THE WRITER IN SOUTH AFRICA

Censorship

What the future holds for South Africa is beyond our comprehension. Questions regarding the present are more accessible: What is it like to be a creative writer or publisher in South Africa today, and what is the literary status of South African writers in exile? *Publishers Weekly* in a special report interviewed a number of persons intimately concerned with publishing in South Africa. Professor A. Coetzee, director of the Directorate of Publications in Cape Town, had this to say: "I hesitate to use the word 'censorship,' because that is the popular term that is used. We call it 'publications control,' because it is not a precensorship system."[1] The other side of this coin is described by Mike Kirkwood, managing director of Raven Press, which has published a number of works critical of apartheid, including John Coetzee's first novel, *Dusklands:* "A publisher loses money *before* a book gets banned because it is frightened to print to the full capacity of the readership. It's really a serious intervention into the development of a culture" ("Out of the Shadows," 27). David Philip, a veteran of thirty years of publishing (including seventeen years at Oxford University Press) observes: "There are tremendous powers available to this government: powers to detain people without trial; powers to censor books, to declare them undesirable." Philip points out that South Africans are subject to a Scylla and Charybdis of governmental control: "There is the Suppression of Communism Act, which bans *people:* you can't publish the works of banned people and you may not quote them, and there is no question of taking a risk—you can't do it. And then there is the Publications Act, which

bans *books*" (27). Of the option available to writers or publishers to submit galleys to the secret committees which designate passages to be deleted or modified, Philip says, "it is quite intolerable for any self-
respecting publisher to submit himself to this kind of prepublication
censorship" (27). Asked in the same interview if censorship affected his
creative process, John Coetzee responded in 1982, "Definitely not. And
I would think that you would get the same answer from any serious
writer in this country. I think you act as if it didn't exist while you're
writing" (29). Four years later, in 1986, Coetzee was less sanguine: "For
the writer the deeper problem is *not* to allow himself to be impaled on
the dilemma proposed by the state, namely either to ignore its obscenities or else to produce representations of them. The true challenge is
how not to play the game by the rules of the state, how to establish
one's own authority, how to imagine torture and death on one's own
terms."[2] There is a suggestion in this statement that the fiction writer
should turn away from the tangible, the evanescent present to draw
from the imagination the kinds of archetypal representations that have
characterized some of Coetzee's works, particularly *Waiting for the Barbarians.* Yet there seems to be in Coetzee a contradictory desire to confront South Africa's present agony with all of the candor that realism
and naturalism can summon, as he did in *Life and Times of Michael K.*
In the same 1986 essay he excoriates censorship generally, journalistic
censorship specifically: "If people are starving, let them starve far away
in the bush, where their thin bodies will not be a reproach. If they have
no work, if they have to migrate to the cities, let there be roadblocks,
let there be curfews, let there be laws against vagrancy, begging, squat-
ting, and let offenders be locked away so that no one has to see or hear
them" ("Dark Chamber," 13).

Politics

Certainly in such a society, there is enormous pressure—from others
if not from oneself—to politicize one's creations. Alan Paton contends
that "it would be very difficult to write a story in South Africa that had
nothing to do with apartheid. It is one compelling factor in your life."[3]
Paton also acknowledges that there is a price to be paid by the creative
artist who becomes a political activist, as he was in the Liberal party
until it was outlawed in 1968. He explains his thirty-year silence as an
author as a consequence of his activism: "You can't be in politics and
write novels, it's impossible. You can write other books but you can't
write novels" (28).

For Coetzee, the emotional stress inherent in such a society produces
another problem, the question of the truthfulness of one's characters
and of oneself. In his lecture on Dostoevsky that I taped in 1984, he

said, "As someone from South Africa, the question of sincerity in particular occupies me because we are in a social/political situation where, for a white person to say, 'Yes, I am for the overthrow of the reigning system,' is a peculiar thing. Because the question is, is the motive behind it a desire to climb onto some historical bandwagon? In other words, how does a person know if he is sincere in a situation like that? How does he know that he is speaking the truth?" In a review of Athol Fugard's *Notebooks, 1960–1977,* Coetzee notes that Fugard, in his attempts to maintain a position as an outsider, came under considerable pressure "from the left to engage himself politically (or rather, since Fugard's art *is* an engaged art, to allow the terms of his engagement to be determined for him by the political struggle)."[4] Ultimately, the central concern of Fugard's notebook entries of the mid-1960s becomes the "question of how to commit himself without losing his identity as an artist"(26). This has clearly been a preoccupation for Coetzee as well, whose nonfiction writings, as we have seen, are often highly politicized, but whose fictional works have been criticized by some critics as being too remotely connected to the present struggle. When I asked Coetzee in the interview if he gave himself or his works any kind of political description, he replied, "No. But I am sure there are plenty of people, particularly in South Africa, who would be very happy to do that."

Environment

Broadening the question beyond politics, we can ask what other aspects of South African life make being a writer there a unique experience. In this respect, Coetzee makes rather wide swings between optimism and pessimism. In an interview in 1978, he remarked, "Let's say that in a way it's easier and more difficult being a writer in South Africa than in West European countries; because there are such gigantic subjects of such unassailable importance facing a writer in South Africa. . . . "[5] Four years later he reaffirmed this view: "Writers from England sometimes say that they are envious of South African writers because they have such major themes to tackle, whereas living in England, at least socially and politically, there don't seem to be such major themes."[6] He has even seen novelistic form and conceptualization affected: "For the South African writer the possible structure of fiction is simpler, much less invention is required, much less massive effort of the imagination than is perhaps required by the European writer. . . . That is the positive side of the situation."[7]

In the same interview, Coetzee stressed cultural insularity, the lack of a significant literary tradition, the inescapable presence of violence and oppression: "I think the negative side is a certain obsessiveness, a certain narrowing of horizons. Perhaps a sense that there is an enor-

mous human variety in the world, much more than merely exists in
South Africa"(8). It is worth noting that William Faulkner had equally
compelling reasons to make the same complaint, as well as most of those
that follow, about being a writer in Oxford, Mississippi. Coetzee has
expressed regret at the lack of an intelligentsia: "There is an intelligentsia, but it's very scattered, and people don't seem to know each
other."[8] Asked about the tradition of letters in his country, he responded, "This is not a great literature and there are no really gigantic
figures in it. . . . I read Nadine Gordimer because I think she's extraordinarily accomplished" (Watson interview, 22). Of course, as Stephen Gray has pointed out, the literary works which derive from an
English cultural world in South Africa are not, and never have been,
part of a closed system.[9] The literary tradition within which Coetzee
and many of his contemporaries write is no less than that of the literature of the Western world. Still the milieu rankles. He complains of
"the lack of civilized conversation. And also the general slackness of
pace. There's very little pressure on anyone to do anything here."[10]

Eleven years later, in his acceptance speech for the Jerusalem Prize
for the Freedom of the Individual in Society (April 1987) Coetzee found
more substantive problems than a lack of civilized conversation. He
stressed the strictures on art in a society whose political system had
produced "deformed and stunted relations between human beings" and
"a deformed and stunted inner life." He concluded that "South African
literature is a literature in bondage. . . . It is a less than fully human
literature. It is exactly the kind of literature you would expect people
to write from prison."[11] Indeed, metaphors of imprisonment and en-
trapment are abundant in contemporary South African writings. Recently, he expressed hopes for an eventual change in the climate in
which South African literature is created: "When the choice is no longer
limited to *either* looking on in horrified fascination as the blows fall *or*
turning one's eyes away, then the novel can once again take as its province the whole of life, and even the torture chamber can be accorded a
place in the design."[12]

In the interviews cited, Coetzee speaks of life in South Africa from
the perspective of one of many authors and citizens from that country.
On other occasions he has conveyed a more personal point of view.
After completing his visiting professorship at the State University of
New York at Buffalo for fall 1986, he returned to the University of
Cape Town in December. In his letter to me of 18 February 1987, he
made the reality of South Africa's censorship laws more vivid than I
had previously perceived them:

I've been back in this country some two months. What is actually happening in
other parts of South Africa is difficult to determine, since the internal censor-

ship is almost total, and foreign-language broadcasts (VOA, BBC) are hampered by restrictions on their journalists here. So I can't give any but the most partial and subjective of impressions. But when students come back next week, at the beginning of the academic year, I should have a chance to hear more.

I received another letter dated 23 April 1987, mentioning his recent trip to accept the Jerusalem Prize for the Freedom of the Individual in Society. The following day, 24 April, marked the beginning of student protest demonstrations at the University of Cape Town against the South African government. These protests would evolve into what the *Chronicle of Higher Education* termed "one of South Africa's most violent confrontations yet between students and policemen at a predominantly white campus."[13] The *Chronicle* reported that "at least ten students were wounded when the police fired birdshot at them, two students were mauled by police dogs, and scores of others were beaten with whips"(44). The demonstrations, at their peak, involved about three thousand, or one-fourth, of the university's students. Most of those participating and arrested were white.

Exile

About two years before this 1987 blood-bath, in August 1985, the government placed the country under a state of emergency in the wake of widespread unrest in the black townships; there were reports of murders, mutilations, and disappearances carried out by white "death squads." Coetzee wrote to me then: "Yes, the situation here is appalling. I veer between anger and hopeless despondency." The question arises as to why John Coetzee, with an international reputation as a novelist and outstanding credentials as a scholar and teacher, chooses to remain at his post at the University of Cape Town when he could easily obtain an attractive position elsewhere. He gave a succinct answer to this question in his letter to me of 5 September 1985, in response to my nominating him for a Chair of Excellence at the University of Tennessee:

I do not need to tell you of the turmoil in this country, turmoil which is reflected in the minds of everyone who lives here. My own feeling is that I want to live here as long as it is possible to do some good, in whatever way I can. As a writer, I don't want to go into exile, if only because I have seen what exile does to writers.

Coetzee's commitment to remain in Cape Town has not been shaken by South African Customs' impounding, then later releasing, two of his books, nor by someone's putting a bullet through the windshield of his car while it was parked and empty.

One may wonder why Coetzee is so adamant against becoming a writer in exile when so many of his compatriots already are. Stephen Gray reports that "by the late 1960's as many as half of South Africa's English-language writers of all colours had been expelled over the borders into an international diaspora."[14] Among the most notable of South Africa's writers-in-exile are Breyten Breytenbach, C. J. Driver, Dan Jacobson, Zakes Mda, Rose Moss, Mbulelo Mzamane, and Sheila Roberts. Exiles Alex La Guma and Bessie Head both recently died; Douglas Reid Skinner has now returned to South Africa.[15] While these authors continued to remember, to be concerned about, and in some cases to write about their native land, as Gray puts it, "the literature of South-Africa-in exile no longer exists in any real sense for those who stayed behind" (2). As Coetzee and Brink state in the introduction to their South African reader, A Land Apart, for the exiles, "history froze when they departed; they can no longer be said to give voice to contemporary South Africa."[16] In his 1974 essay on the novels of Alex La Guma, Coetzee envisioned the isolation and estrangement such an exile must feel: "At his desk he must generalize the idea of an audience from a 'you' to an indefinite 'they.'"[17] As for himself, Coetzee acknowledged, "I would probably feel a certain sense of artificial background construction if I were to write fiction set in another environment."[18]

Setting the question of writing aside, there are clearly other bonds that tie Coetzee to his native land. He felt that the environment of places as disparate as England and Texas were both "alien": "What I missed seemed to be a certain emptiness, empty earth and empty sky. . . . What I also missed was the sound of a language whose nuances I understood" (9). In a 1984 interview he observed, "I do believe that people can only be in love with one landscape in their lifetime. One can appreciate and enjoy many geographies, but there is only one that one feels in one's bones."[19] In this, he seems to echo the feeling of his character, Magda, from In the Heart of the Country: "I am corrupted to the bone with the beauty of this forsaken world" (139).

COETZEE'S NOVELS AND THE CRITICS

The Novels: Countries of the Mind

J. M. Coetzee, the ethical individual, the Afrikaner concerned with injustice, concerned, perhaps, with a degree of guilt for his ancestry, for the history of Afrikaners, or perhaps for the larger history of humankind's banalities of oppression and torture, is *one* person, a person who speaks through essays and interviews, and occasionally in person, in an unmistakably clear voice denouncing the injustices he sees. J. M. Coetzee the teller of tales, the illusionist, fabulist, and wordsmith, creates countries of the mind, where the imagination reigns and refuses to be subservient to history's incessant voices. This is not to say that his fictional works do not convey an ethical vision; they do, but their lack of polemics and the ways in which their forms subvert traditional fictional genres disturb some of Coetzee's readers. Teresa Dovey has made this deconstructive quality and the psychoanalytic theories of Lacan in Coetzee's fiction the central subject of her study.[20]

For example, the second novella in *Dusklands,* "The Narrative of Jacobus Coetzee," initially appears to be in the tradition of the historical adventure novel, descended from Defoe and numerous other eighteenth-century authors. It creates the illusion of an eighteenth-century documentary, attractively packaged with a bogus historical preface and appendices. The protagonist, named after the historical Afrikaner Jacobus Coetzee, at the beginning summons up the atmosphere of the veld across which he travels: "mutton fat and thornbush smoke," Hottentots and Bushmen, the land of the Great Namaqua, but he ends speaking a delirious stream of consciousness that made its most notable appearance first in the pages of James Joyce. The self-indictment of the rapacious colonizing mentality remains solid, but the reader is forced to acknowledge that the historicity is illusionary. Similarly, *In the Heart of the Country,* set on an isolated farm somewhere in the Cape province at the turn of the century, is an inversion of the pastoral genre. Coetzee's novel is concerned throughout with the effects of colonialism and the nature of master/slave relations, but these themes are filtered through the consciousness of a deranged spinster narrator who repeatedly contradicts herself so that the reader can never be sure whether anything he or she has been told is "true." In fact, language itself is presented as the agency of colonization. This is hardly palatable fare for those expecting the preachments against greed and cruelty that characterize most anticolonial fiction.

Waiting for the Barbarians, probably Coetzee's best-known and most highly praised work, is a transmutation of the traditional liberal novels of Alan Paton and Nadine Gordimer (prior to her *Conservationist* [1974]). The protagonist, a magistrate in the service of Empire in a remote outpost in some indiscernible time and place, is an ethical, courageous man who acts on the belief that his individual rebellion against the tyranny of Empire can effect moral changes. His renunciation of the barbarism of Empire is a liberal, humanitarian action, but his belief that such a gesture can change anything dissolves in a mist of Cartesian doubt. Too, the indefiniteness of the setting enhances the allegorical nature of this work while distancing it from the traditional liberal novel designed to address a social or political problem in a specific place and time.

Coetzee's fourth novel, *Life and Times of Michael K*, is set specifically in South Africa in the near future, against a background of civil war, and has as its protagonist one of that country's disenfranchised majority. Michael K, a solitary outsider, rebels against the manipulations of the government's emissaries. Here it would seem, at last, is Coetzee's long-awaited contribution to the literature of protest, a work that confronts the beast of apartheid head on, in the fashion of Fugard and Gordimer, or of Coetzee's essays, for that matter. However, the author has deliberately obscured the race of his protagonist, and Michael K, instead of hurling himself against the barricades or dying heroically under the state's iron boot, simply walks away from everything, searching for a quiet place to be a gardener.

Foe, Coetzee's fifth novel, comes full circle back to the eighteenth-century travel/adventure novel where he began. *Foe* is Coetzee's most reflexive novel, resurrecting and deconstructing Defoe's *Robinson Crusoe* and taking as one of its principal concerns the nature of narrative art. To be sure, the themes of master/slave and the colonial dilemma are there, but they seem so remote from South Africa that they become questions of broad principle. The mute Friday, lacking the articulate force of Fugard's characters, is less a character than a symbol of the silent rage of all those in bondage.

The Critics: Politics and Malaise

Not surprisingly, neo-Marxist critics have raised the greatest outcry over Coetzee's lack of a clear Leftist political stance, his not specifically finding as the *real* villain capitalist materialist economic motives, and perhaps above all, the absence in his book of "solutions" to the problems attendant upon the master/slave, colonial situations which he often portrays. The allegorical *Waiting for the Barbarians* is a case in point. Paul Rich contends that "for neo-Marxist critics this vision of empire has seemed all too simplistic, lacking any understanding of the historical forces that produce actual imperial systems at particular phases of history; failing, above all, to have any understanding of *capitalist* economic processes leading to a capitalist imperialist civilization."[21] Coetzee has not been "able to perceive any moral transcendence of this" (388), which leads Rich to conclude that "literary postmodernism in a post colonial context as South Africa, burdened by the cleavages of race and class and the historical inheritance of Western imperialist control, is a moral dead end" (389).

Michael Vaughan asserts that Coetzee's Afrikaner ancestry circumscribes his ability to see beyond his own cultural heritage: "He is a Coetzee among Coetzees. He too is subject to an ascribed mode of consciousness, that very one proper to the Northern European Protestant type of colonizer-enslaver of his fiction."[22] Thus Coetzee's fictional language "can say next to nothing outside the modality of its own racial-historical dialectic" (128). Vaughan observes that Coetzee has little or no interest in the economic motives of colonialism: "Oppression of the barbarians appears to have no material logic whatsoever, but to be carried through simply for the sake of the *idea* of domination" (137). Like Rich, Vaughan deplores the lack of pragmatic solutions in the novel: "Coetzee thus casts himself in the role of diagnostician of the malady of Western culture who is unable to propose any cure for this malady" (134). Finally, the absence of a clear political strategy in *Barbarians* aroused the ire of what Menan Du Plessis termed "Left-wing student opinion" in a University of Cape Town student publication, which she quotes: "In the end it is not a disturbing book, and ultimately it challenges nothing. Coetzee is a fine writer. It's a pity he isn't a bolder one."[23]

Even those critics who appear to occupy a political middle ground have difficulty accepting the lack of ideological purposefulness in Coetzee's fictions. W.J.B. Wood notes that the predicament of the magistrate in *Barbarians* is presented "in such a way as to make it profoundly moving and disturbing, especially to anyone with liberal humanist proclivities."[24] In an essay on *Dusklands,* Peter Knox-Shaw expresses regret that "a writer of such considerable and varied talents should play down the political and economic aspects of history in favor of a psychopathology of Western life."[25] At the same time, he acknowledges that the novel has broad ramifications in that the old explorer Jacobus Coetzee is a "representative figure not only in the context of Afrikanerdom but of Western culture as well" (78). Rowland Smith accuses Coetzee of avoiding "direct comment on the stalemated horror of the present" saying that he is "too much the knowing outsider almost reveling in his disdain for a farcical, power-drunk world."[26] Smith even goes so far as to assert that Coetzee adopted an interior monologue narrative in *In the Heart of the Country* in order to "comment on the unrelieved gloom of racial confrontation and yet to be dissociated from the moral jungle" he depicts.[27] If there is any implication here that Coetzee lacks moral courage, his essays and public speeches should answer that charge solidly enough.

Beyond the absence of overt political and moral stances, some readers have focused on another quality that is a constant in Coetzee's works. In her review of *Life and Times of Michael K,* Nadine Gordimer concludes: "The sense is of the ultimate malaise: of destruction. Not even the oppressor really believes in what he is doing anymore, let alone the revolutionary."[28] Richard G. Martin, in an essay on *Waiting for the Barbarians,* detects the voice of the " 'sonorous malediction' of an idealistic humanism finding itself in alien territory."[29] This, Martin contends, is the result of a lack of "transcendental order which endows everything with meaning; the significance of every object is its resistance to significance" (15). W.J.B. Wood traces this quality of nontranscendence in Coetzee's fiction (specifically in *Barbarians*) to the impact that Descartes has had on Western philosophy: "Coetzee's work is testimony not so much to a truth about Empire and the legacy of imperial consciousness, as the legacy in alienation that is our Cartesian inheritance."[30] For Lance Olsen, the quality of emptiness, of malaise, in Coetzee's fictions is a positive one, which liberates the reader "by unfolding the repressed, by setting free the absence that dwells in the heart of the country."[31]

The Critics: Colonial Dialectic

These critics are correct in their assertions that while Coetzee's fictions all deal with the circumstances and mentality of colonialism and of master/slave relations, they seldom deal directly with the particulars of the political struggle in South Africa or with the economic factors of colonialism generally. Even *Michael K,* Coetzee's most straightforwardly realistic novel, is set in an imagined near future in the Cape province on the fringes of an armed conflict and far from any centers of power. This work, too, is largely concerned with the inarticulate consciousness of a man who wants most of all to be left alone to be a gardener. The critics are correct in asserting, too, that while Coetzee is often concerned with history from an overview—history as meaning imposed on events, history as a great outflow determining the lives of those in its path—his works are essentially ahistorical: his eighteenth-century Jacobus envisions flame throwers; Magda in the early 1900s seems knowledgeable about structural linguistics. His critics are also right in observing that his novels offer no pragmatic solutions to current affairs, that his characters usually struggle in vain to escape their positions of dominance/submission, and that at the center of his metaphysical world there seems to be an absence, an emptiness.

Stephen Watson, one of Coetzee's colleagues in the English department at the University of Cape Town, addresses these matters in the most perceptive essay on Coetzee's fiction yet to appear. There are two tracks to Watson's thesis: one has to do with Coetzee's circumstance as an English-speaking intellectual living and writing in South Africa, the other concerns Coetzee's particular focus on the origins and essence of colonialism. Coetzee, whose Afrikaner ancestry dates back three hundred years, is in a minority position in his opposition to the beliefs of his fellow Afrikaners regarding apartheid and colonialism. Watson identifies Coetzee as "the colonizer who refuses," quoting from Albert Memmi's *Colonizer and the Colonized:* "It is not easy to escape mentally from a concrete situation, to refuse its ideology while continuing to live with its actual relationships. From now on, he [the colonizer] lives his life under the sign of a contradiction which looms at every step, depriving him of all coherence and all tranquility."[32] That is to say, Coetzee, who chooses to remain in South Africa, acts out of conscience, let us say, to denounce apartheid, colonialism, and the repressive and violent actions of the state. Yet, as a white Afrikaner, he lives in a privileged status in comparison to the destitute multitudes. Also, even if he is personally innocent of any overt misdeeds, he still shares subjective responsibility as a member of the oppressive colonizer group. Many of us share such privilege, such responsibility.

Thus, there are paradoxes—literally, circumstances "beyond thought" —inherent in Coetzee's situation. Like every other person seeking an ethical solution to South Africa's problems, he stands face to face with the awesome presence of three hundred years of colonial history. In a 1984 interview, he commented on Magda's attempt in *In the Heart of the Country* to relinquish her position of mastery and establish a relationship of equality with her servants: "But it fails, and it fails because a mere effort of will is not enough to overcome centuries of cultural and spiritual deformation."[33] Magda, like the magistrate in *Barbarians* and Susan Barton in *Foe,* yearns for a personal circumstance and a society founded in equality, but has little expectation that such will ever come to be. Confronting the Cartesian origins of colonialism in the South African present leads to what Gordimer and others have called the "malaise" or "absence" at the heart of Coetzee's fiction.

Stephen Watson believes that the "colonizer who refuses" is caught in a dilemma, having simultaneous desires to be in the contemplative or creative world of *being* and in the active-participant world of *becoming:*

This type of person is half in the world of being, only half in the world of becoming. They cannot fail to feel the wrench of history pulling them in one direction and, simultaneously, the opposing pull of a world of contemplation where time is cyclical and knows no interruptions. . . . They often cannot decide in favor of one or other mode of being. If they choose contemplation, history will not cease to remind them of their irresponsibility and guilt. If they decide to act, to enter history, the world of being that they have necessarily left behind will continue to be present to them in the form of an inner hollowness. ("Colonialism," 385)

This impasse, in itself, cannot account for the sharp contrast between the portrayals of colonialism in Coetzee's novels and those of other white South African writers. They, too, must face contradictions and dilemmas at the very deepest levels. The source of this fundamental difference has already been noted in W.J.B. Wood's observation that Coetzee's fictions are ultimately about "the legacy in alienation that is our Cartesian inheritance" (*"Waiting for the Barbarians,"* 135). Watson concurs, asserting that Descartes' dualism is at the center of Coetzee's concern: "The colonizing project of the West was set in motion when this same (Western) man embarked upon his Cartesian project of separating subject from object, self from world in a dualism which privileged the first of these two terms and thereby assured his domination of nature and any other obstacle he might confront" ("Colonialism," 375). Thus, Coetzee goes beyond the politics of contemporary South Africa, beyond the material motives of colonialism that the neo-Marxists would have him address, to explore the Cartesian origins of the master/slave mentality, what Watson calls "the metaphysics of power" (389).

This dichotomy is readily apparent in the novels. Jacobus, the explorer-destroyer in *Dusklands,* the archetypal colonizer, never doubts the "otherness" of the Hottentots whom he murders. He justifies the separateness of his tribe from theirs by thinking, "We are Christians, a folk with a destiny" (57). Magda in *In the Heart of the Country* attempts to be "neither master nor slave, neither parent nor child, but the bridge between" and fails (257). The magistrate in *Barbarians,* a colonizer who refuses, is tormented by thoughts that, as a member of Empire, he is as guilty as Empire's sadistic torturers. Even after refuting these doubts, he concludes: "To the last we will have learned nothing. In all of us, deep down, there seems to be something granite and unteachable" (143). The protagonist of *Michael K* is the only one of Coetzee's characters to achieve *being* in Watson's sense, and he does so through "a yielding up of himself to time, to a time flowing slowly like oil from horizon to horizon over the face of the world" (115). He also does so at the cost of removing himself from historical time, withdrawing from society's turmoils. Susan Barton, the spirited and capable narrator of *Foe,* is at a loss to escape her master/slave relationship. Having taken on responsibility for Friday, "a child unborn, a child waiting to be born that cannot be born" (122), she feels that she has become "a beast of burden," and will "stifle" if she cannot be free of him (148). She cannot translate desire into action, however: "But how is Friday to recover his freedom, who has been a slave all his life? That is the true question. Should I liberate him into a world of wolves and expect to be commended for it?" (148). Thus Coetzee, through Barton, voices the present dilemma of colonialism: how to end itself.

Coetzee's novels suggest that reconstituting the colonial consciousness is a task at best difficult, at worst, impossible. In his interview with me he pointed out that "history is an imposition of meaning on time and events, but that time and that meaning are actually linguistic; they are language. So those things are all connected." Watson develops this idea further: "In the way that human relations are opaque and destructive in the colonial situation, so, Coetzee would seem to suggest, language itself fails to signify, to mean at all, under the conditions prevailing in such a situation. The only tongue the colonialist can speak is the circular one of tautology" ("Colonialism," 373).

This theme is especially important in *In the Heart of the Country*. Magda, the deranged spinster, fails in her attempt to bridge the linguistic gulf between herself and the servants, and between herself and her father, who has taken the wife of their "coloured" servant as his lover. Magda is bothered less by the miscegenation than by the possibility that her father has spoken to the woman as an equal, "exchanging forbidden words" (35), thus violating a primary taboo of her colonial upbringing: "Perhaps my rage at my father is simply rage at the violations of the old language, the correct language" (43). Later she says of the "language of hierarchy, of distance and perspective," into which she was born, "I do not say it is the language my heart wants to speak . . . but it is all we have" (97). She never attains the "words of true exchange" (101) she desires, and thus is left a solitary figure, communing with herself in an alien desert she calls home.

What we see in *In the Heart of the Country*, as in all of Coetzee's novels—as different as they may be in form and substance—is a failed dialectic, two opposing points of view that are never resolved in a synthesis. It is this quality that creates the sense of "malaise," of "absence," of "emptiness," that some readers find disturbing or even socially and politically irresponsible on Coetzee's part. My own reading is in agreement with that of Watson, whose comment on *In the Heart of the Country* I would apply to all five novels:

> The novel is surely constructed on the principle that it is through language itself, through those conventional representations which come to be accepted as either "natural" or "universal," that we are colonized as much as by any overt act of physical conquest. The deconstruction of realism, then, is evidently intended, at the most basic level of language itself, as an act of decolonialization and, as such, is very much part of its political meaning. ("Colonialism," 374)

If Coetzee's novels are not seen by some of his readers as being sufficiently relevant to, or specific about, the present turmoil and anguish in South Africa, it is because he addresses a more fundamental question about the cognition and language of worldwide colonialism, of which his own country is one manifestation. Watson states that Coetzee "has provided more insight into the colonizing mind, as well as the dissenting, colonizing mind, than any of his contemporaries" (390). He concludes that Coetzee's novels are distinctive in articulating a desire to end the warped human relationships fostered by colonialism: "Nobody has given a more forceful expression to this hunger, and thereby delivered a more powerful protest against all that the historical phenomenon entails" (390).

NOTES

1. Quoted in Andrew Sussman, "Out of the Shadows: Books in South Africa," *Publishers Weekly* 221 (23 April 1982): 24–30.

2. J. M. Coetzee, "Into the Dark Chamber: The Novelist and South Africa," *New York Times Book Review* 91 (12 January 1986), 13, 35.

3. Quoted in Sussman, "Out of the Shadows," 28.

4. J. M. Coetzee, "Art and Apartheid," *New Republic* 3612 (9 April 1984): 25–28.

5. J. M. Coetzee interview with Stephen Watson, *Speak* 1, no. 3 (1978): 22.

6. J. M. Coetzee quoted in Sussman, "Out of the Shadows," 29.

7. J. M. Coetzee, in interview with Folke Rhedin, *Kunapipi* 6, no. 1 (1984): 8.

8. J. M. Coetzee, in interview with Watson, 22.

9. Stephen Gray, *Southern African Literature: An Introduction* (New York: Harper, 1979), 2.

10. J. M. Coetzee, in interview with Watson, 22.

11. "Coetzee, Getting Prize, Denounces Apartheid," *New York Times,* 11 April 1987, 14.

12. J. M. Coetzee, "Into the Dark Chamber," 35.

13. Helen Zille, "Police Wound Students, Arrest 25 in Protest at South Africa's U.," *Chronicle of Higher Education* (6 May 1987): 44–47.

14. Gray, *Southern African Literature,* 1.

15. *Momentum: On Recent South African Writing,* edited by M. J. Daymond, et. al (Pietermaritzburg, South Africa: Univ. of Natal Press, 1984), 263–312.

16. *A Land Apart: A South African Reader,* edited by André Brink and J. M. Coetzee (London: Faber and Faber, 1986), 8.

17. J. M. Coetzee, "Man's Fate in the Novels of Alex La Guma," *Studies in Black Literature* 5, no. 1 (1974): 16–23.

18. J. M. Coetzee, "How I Learned About America—and Africa—In Texas," *New York Times Book Review,* 9 April 1984, 9.

19. J. M. Coetzee, in interview with Rhedin, 10.

20. Teresa Dovey, *The Novels of J. M. Coetzee: Lacanian Allegories.* Human Sciences Research Council Publication Series, no. 86 (Johannesburg: Ad. Donkor, 1988).

21. Paul Rich, "Apartheid and the Decline of Civilization Idea: An Essay on Nadine Gordimer's *July's People* and J. M. Coetzee's *Waiting for the Barbarians*," *Research in African Literatures* 15, no. 3 (1984): 365–93.

22. Michael Vaughan, "Literature and Politics: Currents in South African Writing in the Seventies," *Journal of South African Studies* 9, no. 1 (1982): 118–38.

23. Quoted in Menan Du Plessis, "Towards a New Materialism," *Contrast* 13, no. 4 (1983): 77–87.

24. W.J.B. Wood, *"Waiting for the Barbarians:* Two Sides of Imperial Rule and Some Related Considerations," in *Momentum,* edited by M. J. Daymond, et. al, (Pietermaritzburg, South Africa: Univ. Natal Press, 1984), 129.

25. Peter Knox-Shaw, *"Dusklands:* A Metaphysics of Violence," *Commonwealth Novel in English* 14, no. 1 (1983): 65–81.

26. Roland Smith, "Allan Quatermain to Rosa Burger: Violence in South African Fiction," *World Literature Written in English* 22, no. 2 (1983), 171–82.

27. Roland Smith, "The Seventies and After," in *Olive Schreiner and After: Essays on Southern African Literature in Honor of Guy Butler,* edited by Malvern Van Wyk Smith and Don Maclennan (Cape Town: David Philip, 1983), 196–204, 233.

28. Nadine Gordimer, "The Idea of Gardening," review of *Life and Times of Michael K,* by J. M. Coetzee, *New York Review of Books,* 2 February 1984, 3, 6.

29. Richard G. Martin, "Narrative, History, Ideology: A Study of *Waiting for the Barbarians* and *Burger's Daughter,"* *Ariel* 17, no. 3 (July 1986): 3–21.

30. Wood, *"Waiting for the Barbarians,"* 135.

31. Lance Martin Olsen, "The Presence of Absence: Coetzee's *Waiting for the Barbarians,"* *Ariel* 16, no. 2 (April 1985): 44–56.

32. Albert Memmi, *The Colonizer and the Colonized* (London: Souvenir Press, 1974), 20; quoted in Stephen Watson, "Colonialism and the Novels of J. M. Coetzee," *Research in African Literatures* 17 (1986), 378.

33. J. M. Coetzee, in interview with Rhedin, 7.

3

Dusklands: The Colonial Will to Power

"THE VIETNAM PROJECT": MYTHOGRAPHICAL MAYHEM

Coetzee's Debut

When John Coetzee returned to Cape Town from the United States in 1971, he had completed approximately half of the manuscript that would become his first novel, *Dusklands*[1] While this first work did not generate the worldwide attention that his later novels would, South African critics accorded it considerable acclaim. W.J.B. Wood regarded it as "a remarkable and distinguished novel that . . . confronts the reader with the need for . . . engaging critically in the recharting of the myths of our culture."[2] Jonathan Crewe found it a "very remarkable book, written with a fastidiousness and power that are rare on the South African literary scene, or any literary scene."[3] Crewe made a pronouncement often quoted by subsequent reviewers: "In *Dusklands* the modern novel in English arrives in South Africa for the first time" (90). Stephen Watson appropriately suggests that Crewe should have specified " 'modernist' or 'postmodernist' novel," but he is no less enthusiastic, associating Coetzee's techniques with those of Borges and Nabokov: "Never before had a South African novel broken so obviously, even self-consciously, with the conventions of realism and so candidly announced its own artificiality, its own fictionality."[4] To those surfeited on a diet of South African liberal realism, Watson concludes: "J. M. Coetzee's first novel had something of the liberating, clarifying force of a genuine revelation" (372). Among the few dissenting voices were the authors of the critical anthology *Perspectives on South African Fiction*, who assert: "The suspicion remains that the unity of *Dusklands* is too shallow, too easily borrowed from the Laingian bomb-in-the-head syndrome. . . . The novel is so solipsistic, so keenly its own peculiar and startling revelation, that, if we follow the strict logic of the situation, 'nobody' wrote it and, perhaps 'nobody' reads it."[5]

Dusklands is two *nouvelles,* "The Vietnam Project" and "The Narrative of Jacobus Coetzee," conjoined by the common theme of colonial oppression and the use of the name *Coetzee* in each. In part I, set in the United States during the Vietnam era, the narrator's bureaucratic supervisor is named Coetzee. In part II, set in the South African interior during the eighteenth century, J. M. Coetzee is presented as the "translator," and his "father," Dr. S. J. Coetzee, as the editor of an "historical" document (the *nouvelle*) presumably written by Jacobus Coetzee. Jacobus is a fictional creation of the "real" J. M. Coetzee, based on his distant historical ancestor, Jacobus Coetzee. Coetzee's use of his surname in the narratives and his inclusion of other self-reflexive devices (to be discussed in part II) call the reader's attention to the fictionality of the work.

The substantive events of *Dusklands* can be summarized as follows: In part I, Eugene Dawn, a U.S. specialist in psychological warfare, dispassionately formulates propaganda designed to render the North Vietnamese impotent to the military might of the United States. Dawn's extreme Cartesian isolation of "I" from the "Other" eventually erupts in a psychotic break in which he stabs his son, symbolically wounding himself. Part II, set approximately two hundred years earlier, is narrated by the South African adventurer Jacobus Coetzee, who emotionlessly describes the most efficient techniques for slaughtering the Namaqua and other South African tribes. Suffering from the same schism between "I" and "Other" that shattered Dawn, Jacobus also undergoes a psychotic upheaval in which he outsavages the savages and, in a murderous rage, wreaks bloody havoc upon some Namaqua who humiliated him. Whereas Dawn ends his narrative with "high hopes of finding out whose fault I am" (49), Jacobus concludes his tale with exuberant self-righteousness.

"The Vietnam Project," like *Foe,* does not offer direct correlations to historical or contemporary South Africa. It is bound to its companion piece and to Coetzee's other works by its exploration of the mentality of colonialism. When asked by Stephen Watson about the period from 1965 to 1971 when he was living in the United States, Coetzee replied, "The major emotional involvement, from a political point of view, was not with the South African situation but with the war in Vietnam," adding an observation quoted earlier, that he sees the South African situation as "only one manifestation of a wider historical situation to do with colonialism, late colonialism, neo-colonialism" (Watson interview, 23). In a reminiscence about his graduate work in the United States,

Coetzee recalled a friend saying to him, " 'If you dislike the war so much,' meaning the war in (on?) Vietnam, 'why don't you leave? There is nothing keeping you here.' But he misread me. Complicity was not the problem—complicity was far too complex a notion for the time being—the problem was with knowing what was being done. It was not obvious where one went to escape knowledge."[6] For Coetzee, a South African citizen and Fulbright scholar working on a Ph.D. at the University of Texas, the question of the degree of his moral responsibility for the Vietnam war must have seemed remote in comparison with his identity as an Afrikaner and his perception of his complicity in colonialism in South Africa. But living in a colonizing country other than his own surely broadened Coetzee's perspective. In 1985 he remarked, "In all my novels, except *From the Heart of the Country,* war comes into the picture and is, of course, a reference to the civil war tearing South Africa apart. But war is also a historical metaphor. Violence does not exist only in my country."[7]

The following analysis of "The Vietnam Project" will focus on four topics: the protagonist's resemblance to Dostoevsky's Underground man, his obsession with phallic dominance, and Coetzee's use of symbolic photographs and mythology to delineate the colonizing mentality. "The Vietnam Project" opens with a quotation from Herman Kahn, the former Rand Corporation consultant, defense strategy advisor to the Pentagon, and popularizer of the "megadeath" concept:

Obviously it is difficult not to sympathize with those European and American audiences who, when shown films of fighter-bomber pilots visibly exhilarated by successful napalm bombing runs on Viet-Cong targets, react with horror and disgust. Yet, it is unreasonable to expect the U.S. Government to obtain pilots who are so appalled by the damage they may be doing that they cannot carry out their missions or become excessively depressed or guilt-ridden.

Kahn's statement establishes one of the major themes of *Dusklands,* and indeed, of most of Coetzee's works: the failed dialectic, the distinct realms of consciousness which separate those who reject murder on ethical grounds from those who concentrate upon the most effective techniques for achieving dominance.

Coetzee's Underground Manqué

"The Vietnam Project" is, like Dostoevsky's *Notes from Underground,* an extended interior monologue. The narrator, Eugene ("well-born") Dawn, is an introverted, intense young theorist in the mythography section of a Rand-type corporation which supplies advice on propaganda to the United States Department of Defense. He is excruciatingly unhappy: his relationship with his wife is emotionally dead; he is at cross-purposes with his supervisor, Coetzee; and he describes himself and his colleagues as Leibnizian "monads," working in isolated glass cubicles to discourage their eccentricities (31). Although the question of literary "influence" is always nebulous, there are some strong echoes of Dostoevsky's protagonist in *Notes from Underground* (1864) in Dawn, as well as some striking contrasts.

When Coetzee came to Lexington in 1984, he gave a lecture on confessional elements in Dostoevsky's fiction, primarily in *The Idiot* (1868–69) but also in *Notes from Underground*. Parts of the lecture were later incorporated in Coetzee's lengthy essay published the following year, "Confession and Double Thoughts: Tolstoy, Rousseau, Dostoevsky." On the day following the lecture, I asked Coetzee about the possibility that his conception of the character Eugene Dawn had been affected by Dostoevsky's protagonist in *Notes from Underground*. Coetzee seemed dubious but acknowledged, "I remember I taught it several years in the sixties and it is quite possible it has left its mark on my 'Vietnam Project.' " Setting the question of influence aside, a comparison of the two characters can be instructive.

The Underground man's famous opening words—"I am a sick man . . . I am a spiteful man. I am an unpleasant man. I think my liver is diseased"[8]—are paralleled in Eugene Dawn's self-description: "There is no doubt that I am a sick man" (32). "My health is poor. I have a treacherous wife, an unhappy home, unsympathetic superiors. I suffer from headaches. I sleep badly" (29). Both characters labor under the delusion that they do not really exist, that they are invisible to others. Underground's sense of self is so precarious that he actually envies a man whom he sees thrown out of a billiard hall window. He decides to go inside the hall himself and provoke an argument so that he, too, can be thrown out of a window, but to his humiliation, he is simply moved aside as though he did not exist. Similarly, Eugene Dawn observes: "The word has been passed around that I do not exist. . . . But I do not go away. If they refuse to see me I will become the ghost of their corridors, the one who rings the telephones, who does not flush the toilet" (32–33).

In addition to their parallel introversion, hyperconsciousness, suffering, and lack of sense of self, Dostoevsky's Underground man and Coetzee's Eugene Dawn are in rebellion against common philosophical opponents: rationalists who posit that self-interest is the ultimate key to all human motivation. Underground asks:

Oh tell me, who first declared, who first proclaimed, that man only does nasty things because he does not know his own real interest; and that if he were enlightened, if his eyes were opened to his real normal interests, man would at once cease to do nasty things, would at once become good and noble because, being enlightened and understanding his real advantage, he would see his own advantage in the good and nothing else, and we all know that not a single man can knowingly act to his own disadvantage.(18)

Both Underground and Dawn are in rebellion against the rationalistic theory of self-interest because it reduces the individual to a cipher, a mechanical piano key, an organ stop. Dawn's reading of his supervisor Coetzee is that "he starts with the axiom that people act identically if their self-interests are identical. His career has been built on the self and its interests. He thinks of me, even me, as merely a self with interests. He cannot understand a man who experiences his self as an envelope holding his body-parts together while inside it he burns and burns" (32). His supervisor Coetzee, in short, is in Dawn's view, "a man who does not believe in magic" (3).

Beyond the preceding parallels, the central characters and themes of Dostoevsky's and Coetzee's *nouvelles* diverge. Dostoevsky's work was a refutation of Russia's rationalistic social theorists of the 1860s, who held that man had no special nature, that free will and religion were an illusion, and that science and economic self-interest were the final measure of all things (Matlaw, Introduction, *Notes from Underground*, vii–xii). Coetzee's work, in contrast, is principally a refutation of the rationale of colonial/phallic dominance. For Dostoevksy, every act of reason was a covert act of will. Absolute freedom of choice was the real interest of man. Thus, Underground rebels against the rationalistic social planners and deliberately makes choices to his own disadvantage to assert his individuality.[9] As Coetzee observes, "The primal desire [for Underground] is therefore the desire for a freedom which the hero identifies with unique individuality."[10]

Ultimately, Dostoevsky's tormented character confesses that making choices to his own disadvantage is a lie, that what he really seeks is something "quite different" from his underground life. Although the Russian censors deleted the key passages, Dostoevsky makes it clear in his personal correspondence and in his other writing that what Underground needed was faith in Christ (Matlaw, Introduction, *Notes from Underground*, xvi).

Coetzee, who holds no brief for either irrational or religious solutions, gives quite a different reading to the character of Underground:

How does the subject know that the choices he makes, even "perverse" choices that bring him no advantage, are truly undetermined? How does he know he is not the slave of a pattern of perverse choices (a pathological pattern, perhaps) whose design is visible to everyone but him? . . . the possibility exists that the truth he tells about himself (the perverse truth, the truth as a story of

perverse "free" choices he has made) might itself be a perverse truth, a perverse choice made in accord with a design invisible to him though perhaps
visible to others ("Confession," 220).

Coetzee offers no Dostoevskian antirational or religious solutions to
his Eugene Dawn. Ironically, Dawn fashions a narrow behavioristic philosophy for himself from the rationalism he has rejected. Dawn concludes that "everything is on the surface and visible in mere behavior,
to those who have eyes to see" (10). Again, "all faults of character are
faults of upbringing" (44). If the essence of humanity can be reduced
to a strict behaviorism, then order and conditioning become the primary virtues, making compassion irrelevant:

If you are moved by the courage of those who have taken up arms, look into
your heart: an honest eye will see that it is not your best self which is moved.
The self which is moved is treacherous. It craves to kneel before the slave, to
wash the leper's sores. The dark self strives toward humiliation and turmoil,
the bright self toward obedience and order. The dark self sickens the bright
self with doubts and qualms. I know (27).

In a reductio ad absurdum reminiscent of Gogol's central character in
"Diary of a Madman," Dawn concludes: "I think that an alphabetic or-
dering of the world will in the end turn out to be superior to the other
orderings people have tried" (30). As Dawn observes in his contribution
to the "New Life" propaganda report, "Questions of conscience lie outside the purview of this study" (22). The conflict between those who
would order and dominate and those who would understand and suc-
cor is a prominent theme in Coetzee's subsequent novels.

Cyclops Evades the Enemy's Eye

We have already noted that Stephen Watson sees the central thesis
of Coetzee's fiction as the examination of the "Cartesian project of separating subject from object, self from world" ("Colonialism," 375). Dawn
observes that the propaganda voice broadcast into Vietnamese homes
is "the voice of the doubting self, the voice of René Descartes driving
his wedge between the self in the world and the self who contemplates
that self" (20). As Watson says, colonialism as perceived by Coetzee is
"primarily the projection of a certain mental aberration located exclusively in the divided consciousness that is a special feature of Western
humanity" ("Colonialism," 375). For Dawn, as for Jacobus, this aberration manifests itself in fantasies of phallic dominance that are intrinsi-
cally connected with colonial dominance.

Dawn's monologue is rife with images of sexual/political dominance and subjection. In describing his attempts at sexual intercourse with his wife, Marilyn, he addresses her in his thoughts: "When for my part I convulse your body with my little battery-driven probe, I am only finding a franker way to touch my own centers of power than through the unsatisfying genital connection. (She cries when I do it but I know she loves it. People are all the same)" (10). The sexual images easily merge with death images as Dawn thinks of the Vietnamese: "We brought with us weapons, the gun and its metaphors, the only copulas we knew of between ourselves and our objects. . . . We forced ourselves deeper than we had ever gone before into their women; but when we came back we were still alone, and the women like stone" (17–18). The ultimate question for Dawn is: "How can we make our programs more penetrant?" (20). Or, as one critic put it: "Why are we in Vietnam? We are testing our authenticity against their otherness, trying out 'probes of reality,' bullets, phalluses, fruit knives, journeys, words on paper" (*Perspectives*, 178).

Dawn's sadistic, phallic attitudes toward his wife and the North Vietnamese are but part of his larger revulsion for humanity generally and the earth itself. To portray this revulsion, Coetzee uses descriptions of symbolic photographs (as he later uses symbolic dreams in *In the Heart of the Country* and *Waiting for the Barbarians*). In his briefcase Dawn carries with him twenty-four well-guarded photographs depicting atrocities from the Vietnamese war. His wife correctly intuits that her husband has a "secret, a cancer of shameful knowledge" (10), even though she never sees the pictures. The reader is given a description of only three of these, but they convey poignantly the end results of colonial phallic dominance. The triptych includes one photograph of sexual abuse, a central depiction of murder, and a third panel of imprisonment and torture. This unholy trinity opens with a picture of a former linebacker (6'2", 220 lbs.) from the football team of the University of Houston copulating with a thin, fragile Vietnamese woman whom he has lifted aloft on his erect penis, his hands braced on his own buttocks. Eugene Dawn has tentatively entitled this photograph, "Father Makes Merry with Children" (13). Through Dawn's ironic, flippant statement, Coetzee emphasizes the horror of the central panel, which portrays two U.S. Special Forces sergeants, whose nametags read Berry (bury) and Wilson (will-son), who hold before them the severed heads of three Vietnamese men. The horror resides not so much in the grisly display as in Dawn's mocking, dispassionate rhetoric: "it is heartening to see that, marmoreally severe, these faces are as well-defined as the faces of sleepers, and their mouths decently shut. They have died well. (Nevertheless, I find something ridiculous about a severed head . . . even a man-size plastic bag may have its elemental dignity; but can one say the same of a mother with her son's head in a sack, carrying it off like a small purchase from the supermarket? I giggle" (15–16).

The third print differs from the first two in that it is a still photograph taken from a propaganda motion picture film depicting North Vietnamese soldiers imprisoned in tiger cages on Hon Tre Island. The movie provides a panoramic context: a walled prison courtyard, rows of identical concrete pits with wire mesh grates, an officer gesturing toward *one* cage, and finally, a closeup still of the face of the man in the cage. The propinquity of the face provides Dawn with the potential to see the man as a human being rather than as just another grotesque photographic joke. Momentarily, it seems that Dawn will bridge the gap to understanding as he observes the details of the man's body raised on one elbow, his eyes dazzled by the light, the thinness of his face, one eye reflecting a point of light, the other shadowed by the darkness of the cage. This is the moment of truth—for compassion or the failure of compassion. An instructive observation is made by Graham Greene's "whiskey priest" in *The Power and the Glory:* "When you visualize a man or woman carefully, you could always begin to feel pity . . . when you saw the lines at the corners of the eyes, the shape of the mouth, how the hair grew, it was impossible to hate. Hate was just a failure of the imagination."[11] Similarly, the magistrate in *Waiting for the Barbarians* is filled with hatred for the sadist, Colonel Joll, and wishes to drag his body through jagged glass, but then perceives Joll's "pale high temples" and imagines Joll's "memories of his mother's soft breast, of the tug in his hand of the first kite he ever flew, as well as those intimate cruelties" which Joll inflicted on the native population (146). Through his willed imagination, the magistrate overcomes the hatred that arises from the vast ethical gulf that separates him from Joll. Dawn has no desire to overcome the distance between himself and the Other in the photograph. Rather, he applauds himself "for having kept away from the physical Vietnam" (16). He prefers the flat image of the photograph: "Everywhere its surface is the same" (16). The moment when the eye in the photograph will look into his eye is a "moment luckily never to arrive" (16). He is content to be ensconced in his solipsistic solitude: "My true ideal (I really believe this) is of an endless discourse of character, the self reading the self to the self in all infinity" (38).

Metamyths

The brief second section of "The Vietnam Project" consists of Dawn's report to his superior, Coetzee, concerning his propaganda recommendations for the ironically titled "New Life Project." The narrative style changes radically here; gone are the subjectivism and erratic emotionalism of the hyperconscious Underground man; in its place is the terse bureaucratese of the official propagandist. The goal of Dawn's report is phallic dominance—how to make U.S. propaganda more "penetrant" in Vietnam. The method is to associate the U.S. propaganda voice with the mythic Vietnamese concept of father: "authority, infallibility, ubiquity. He does not persuade, he commands" (21).

In the traditional Vietnamese myth (which closely parallels the Uranus–Cronus myth), the sons rebel, mutilate the father, and fertilize the earth with the "father's rain" (25). In Dawn's application of the myth to Vietnam, the sons are the brotherhood of earth-tillers who want to take the land for themselves by overthrowing the sky-god (U.S. bombers); the earth-mother conceals the sons from the "thunderbolts" of the father; at night while he sleeps, the sons unman him. Dawn must revise the traditional myth because it makes the father vulnerable. His point of attack is against the idea that the earth-mother and sky-father live in symbiosis, and that neither can exist alone. His solution is to dispose of the earth-mother by means of what he terms "meta-historical consciousness" (26). History had made the earth expendable; her sons no longer till the earth but devour and destroy her. Our explorations of space lead us to "new celestial loves": "Our future belongs not to the earth but to the stars" (29). The end of the tellurian age is at hand. Despite his apocalyptic fervor, Dawn has presented a fair assessment of the way the powers of the nuclear age regard the earth and the way the colonizing mentality has traditionally regarded the Other.

In his perceptive study of Coetzee's fiction, Jan Haluska gives a metaphoric interpretation of the mythology of "The Vietnam Project," based in part on Dawn's statement that "the Vietnam report has been composed facing the east into the rising sun in a mood of poignant regret (*poindre*, to pierce) that I am rooted in evening lands" (6). Haluska observes:

Although rooted in night, the dawn itself faces an eastern future, and exists only in the ephemeral moments before actual sunrise. The sun, as traditionally godlike ruler of the earth, is a fitting symbol for the omnipotent father/master whom Dawn reports as advancing just over the horizon, while he himself seems bound in the twilight of ambivalence as an obedient, orderly son awaiting the full glare of dominion, while yet cherishing shadowy rebellion in his heart.[12]

Thus, in Haluska's reading, Dawn is both master and slave: a would-be master to the people he wishes to conquer, and a slave to the colonizing masters whom he serves.

Loco Motel

In the third section of "The Vietnam Project," Dawn becomes increasingly paranoid and hypochondriacal: "Sometimes I think the wound is in my stomach, that it bleeds slime and despair over the food that should be nourishing me, seeping in little puddles that rot the crooks of my obscurer hooked organs" (32). In the fourth section, he rescues himself from a slough of despair, like Underground man before him, by finally *acting:* "I marvel at myself. I have done a deed" (35). Dawn's deed is to have achieved a full-fledged psychotic episode in which he spirits his son Martin away to a small town in California where they take a room in the appropriately named Loco Motel. There Dawn attains "the rapture of pure contemplation . . . drenched in reverie and waiting for something to happen" (38). The language that he uses to describe his malady suggests that its source is his involvement in the destruction of the Vietnamese people: "It is a thing, a child not mine, once a baby squat and yellow whelmed in the dead center of my body, sucking my blood, growing by my waste, now, 1973, a hideous mongol boy who stretches his limbs inside my hollow bones, gnaws my liver . . . and will not go" (39). In his delirium he apparently confuses the "mongol boy" with his son, whom he stabs with a fruit-knife as the police close in to arrest him. The act is also symbolically an act of self-destruction, for Dawn observes that he has injured his "own flesh and blood" (44).

The final segment finds Dawn in a mental institution where, like Camus' *Le Renégat,* he longs for order, the "order that is going to make me well again" (46). He does not communicate with his wife and son; rather, he is having a love affair with words—"I live in them and they in me—and with his room—"it is part of my cure to learn to form stable attachments" (43). His analysts have hypothesized that his breakdown was a result of his involvement with the Vietnam war. One might further connect Dawn's psychological condition with the state of mind of U.S. society generally during and following the Vietnam era. Dawn says that he attempted "to impose order on an area of chaos" because he wanted to end the guilt that the war was creating: "Guilt was entering our homes through the TV cables. We ate our meals in the glare of that beast's glass eye from the darkest corner" (48). In his parting words to the reader, Dawn anticipates working through his entire childhood, beginning with his "vampire" mother and soldier father. He has "high hopes" of finding out whose fault he is.

It is appropriate at this point to assess Coetzee's artistic accomplishment in "The Vietnam Project." In my interview with him, he remarked that the composition of *"Dusklands* took a long time, because I was feeling my way. It took over three years." In this, his first, his apprenticeship *nouvelle,* Coetzee seems less at ease with characterization and style than in his later works, including the second part of *Dusklands.* The presentation of monomaniacal Dawn's political obsessions at times becomes labored. In "The Narrative of Jacobus Coetzee," Jacobus's mad ethnocentrism and megalomania are woven into the palpable textures of the eighteenth-century South African landscape, and of the cultures of the Hottentot and Namaqua. In "The Vietnam Project," Coetzee offers little more by way of a tangible setting than perfunctory references to the "Harry S. Truman Library" and the "Loco Motel." There is no concrete sense of "America," as, for example, in Nabokov's *Lolita*. Also, whereas Jacobus's servants emerge as distinct, individual characters, in Dawn's monologues, the Others, including his supervisor, his wife, and his son, are simply shadows of Dawn's obsessions. The aesthetic strength of "The Vietnam Project," I believe, is to be found in Coetzee's use of the vividly haunting war photographs and in his skillful interweaving of mythological themes.

"THE NARRATIVE OF JACOBUS COETZEE": PSYCHIC JOURNEY TO THE HEART OF DARKNESS

The Colonial Connection

The narrator-protagonist of the second *nouvelle* of *Dusklands*, Jacobus Coetzee, is, as noted earlier, a remote ancestor of the author. (For clarity, I shall refer to the author as Coetzee and to his character as Jacobus.) Jacobus—physically aggressive, supremely self-confident, and self-righteous—is a foil to doubting, introspective Eugene Dawn. The two characters can be seen as representatives of their respective eras of colonialism, as Michael Vaughan suggests: Dawn the contemporary intellectual enmeshed in the "doom-laden projects of latter-day imperialism," and Jacobus "the early explorer-colonizer, living out the anarchic individualism of . . . the youthful vigour of Western imperialism." And yet, Vaughan adds, "they are identical, not in character or experience, but in the mode of *consciousness* by which they perceive their world, and their relation to this world."[13] That is to say, each operates within the bounds of the Cartesian separation of Self from Other, and each is obsessed with the technology of domination: "The treatment of North Vietnamese and Namaquas is exactly the same—the gun is God, after all."[14]

Coetzee's use of history will be discussed later in conjunction with the reflexive nature of this narrative. Suffice it to say now that the historical Jacobus Coetzee was a South African hunter and explorer living in the Western Cape in the 1760s who believed himself to be the first European to discover the Orange River and who brought his countrymen information about the interior.[15] This historical connection, however, is primarily a starting point for Coetzee's creation of a paradoxical and dynamically evolving fictive character. In the beginning, Jacobus is a rather unexceptional eighteenth-century Afrikaner lacking in self-

awareness and intent upon carrying out the dual colonial goals of dominance and acquisition. Whereas the hyperconscious Eugene Dawn is
finally undone by his guilt over his contribution to the murder of Vietnamese, Jacobus Coetzee seems totally unaware that his attitude toward
the indigenous peoples of Africa is in any way barbaric. He assumes a
sympathetic audience and adopts the emotionless, pragmatic style of a
military field guide: "The only sure way to kill a bushman is to catch
him where your horse can run him down. . . . The only one I ever
caught on foot was an old woman up in the mountains . . . too old
and sick to walk" (58–59). As with Dawn, Jacobus's primary concern is
with methodology. How to hunt Hottentots: "The technique is to ride
down on your man till you are just outside arrow range, then pull up
quickly, sight, and fire. If you are lucky he will still be running and it
is an easy shot in the back" (59). He speaks admiringly of the ingenuity
of an Afrikaner farmer who rigged a trip-string to a shotgun near a
Bushman watering place and succeeded in blowing the face off of a
male and wounding a female so badly she could not move. The farmer
later hung the bodies as human scarecrows. However, shooting is not
the preferred method. It is better, Jacobus suggests, to follow the example of the hunting party who caught a Bushman and "tied him over
a fire and roasted him. They even basted him in his own fat. Then they
offered him to the Hottentots; but he was too sinewy, they said, to eat"
(60).

Whereas Dawn refused to consider any questions of morality, Jacobus counters any potential ethical objections with the argument, noted
earlier, that his tribe is divinely favored: "The one gulf that divides us
from the Hottentots is our Christianity. We are Christians, a folk with
a destiny" (57). The Christianity of converted Hottentots does not count.
The effect of such conversions is to turn a reliably predictable savage
into a deceitful "false creature" in "Christian clothes" (65). Moreover,
as Coetzee points out in another context, "the Afrikaner Calvinist
churches have long taught that the division of mankind into ethnic types
is part of God's dispensation, and that deliberately to confuse or to
transgress these God-given boundaries is an act of disobedience."[16]

Psychic Journey

At the beginning of his journey north with six Hottentots, Jacobus is
supremely confident of his superiority. It is he, he tells us, who planned
each day's march, conserved the oxen, provided the food, and main-
tained order among his charges: "They saw me as their father. They
would have died without me" (64). When they reach a village of Namaqua people, his self-importance reaches its pinnacle: "Perhaps on
my horse and with the sun over my right shoulder I looked like a god,

a god of the kind they did not have yet. The Hottentots are a primitive people" (71). Worse, "they lacked all will, they were born slaves" (73–74). As he waits for their chieftain to receive him with ceremonial rituals, he imagines that he looks like an "equestrian statue" (72).

Jacobus's fall from these lofty heights is precipitous. While he is picturing himself as a bronzed horseman, he realizes that a group of mocking Hottentot boys are calling him "Long-Nose." The "chief" turns out to be a sick, dying old man, to whom Jacobus gives tobacco, a tinderbox, and wire, assuming this to be proper protocol. While he is doing so, the villagers ransack his goods; when he threatens them with his rifle, they "hiss" at him. Meanwhile, a fat woman shakes her naked breasts at him in derision. To complete his humiliation, he becomes a kind of perverse Job, developing a huge carbuncle near his anus, accompanied by a high fever. His survival now depends on the good will of the Namaqua, who quarantine him in one of the huts ordinarily occupied by menstruating women.

Dovey gives an instructive reading of the preceding events:

In the context of the narrative self's confrontation with the Other, the strange Hottentot tribe functions as a kind of cultural silence, a nothingness, a void. In its apparent absence of organization and ritual, it is one with the infinitely receding space which offers no resistance to Jacobus Coetzee's advance, and so provides no proof of his identity.[17]

Jacobus's desperate need to re-establish his identity takes him on a psychedelic journey in which the explorer of unkown lands becomes an explorer of his own unexamined interiority. The journey begins with an hallucination of his deceased mother reading about his death and evolves into an apocalyptic revelation confirming his existence and beliefs. In his first vision, a sun-dazzled stone desert speaks to him "from its stone heart to mine," telling him that behind every exterior there lies a "black interior quite, quite strange to the world" (77). Yet when any interior is penetrated (as with a hammer smashing a stone) the interior transforms itself into exterior, so that there is no certainty that interiors exist. Jacobus reflects that "Entombed in its coffer my heart too had lived in darkness all its life" (78). He speculates that all of his life may have been dream and that if he were to awaken from it, he might be in a universe in which "I the Dreamer" would be the sole inhabitant. This echoes Dawn's solipsistic ontology, as well as Western philosophy's turning inward, along with Descartes, to confirm its own existence.

In another vision, he is an environment of space and solitude pervaded by sun. His senses—all but sight—are in a vacuum: "I became a spherical eye moving through the wilderness and ingesting it. . . . I am all that I see. Such loneliness! . . . What is there that is not me?" In stoic finality, he concludes that he is a "transparent sac with a black core full of images and a gun" (79). With a convoluted logic, he perceives the gun to be "our savior" because, by producing death, it gives evidence of life and saves us from "the fear that all life is within us" (79). He views the carnage of the animals he has killed as his "dispersed pyramid to life" (79). Reflecting that a gun is useless in annihilating trees and bushes, he imagines some kind of "flame-throwing device" (coupling him with Eugene Dawn's Vietnam). The need for the gun, he concludes, is metaphysical rather than physical. The gun produces the death of the hare, which is Jacobus's "metaphysical meat" because it keeps his "soul from merging with the world" (79–80). He reasons that he must also kill the Hottentot because "he threatens to have a history in which I shall be a term. Such is the material basis of the malady of the master's soul" (81).

Jacobus's psychic journey can be interpreted as follows: The solitary mastering soul maintains its interior in a depth of darkness unknown to the Others. When its interior is revealed to light, it can no longer exist in solitary darkness. Brought up from the depths, it is exposed to a brilliance of light that is blinding, and then, to all that the light illumines. The soul, an Eye, at first perceives all that is illumined to be part of the soul's dream, to be part of the soul itself. Then separateness occurs to the dreamer. What the soul perceives is not I, but the Others. The dream of union is shattered with a blast of thought, and of a gun. The solitary soul asserts its mastery over the Other, and the paradoxical relationship of master and slave is born. This is the heart of the paradox that all of Coetzee's fiction explores.

Jacobus's delirium gradually subsides, and he begins to regain his strength and senses, but he finds that he has lost his position of mastery over his servants. Only fifty-year-old Klawer, who had shared his boyhood with Jacobus, remains loyal, because the "habit of obedience is not easily broken" (88).

Before he leaves the village with Klawer, Jacobus undergoes a ritual emersion that marks a transformation in him, a kind of reverse acculturation in which he divests himself of his gloss of civilization and becomes increasingly savage. During his infirmity, he regards his carbuncle as a companion as well as a disease: "it still yielded a pleasant itch. Thus I was not quite alone" (83). He once refers to it as his "offspring," and admires its stubbornness. Rather like the Beckett character who so relishes his pains that he prays to the "Omnidolent,"[18] Jacobus goes to a stream where he squeezes his "pus-knob" and experiences erotic "climax after climax of pain." He reflects: "Such must be the gratifications of the damned" (89). Immediately following this purging, he savagely attacks a group of boys who stole his clothes as a joke: "Roaring like a lion and enveloped in spray like Aphrodite I fell upon them" (90). He catches one of the boys, grinds his face into stones, kicks him, curses him, and in the melee that follows, comes up with hair and a human ear in his mouth. The villagers, shocked at such barbarism, chastise him for mutilating a child and banish him from the village.

Jacobus, never one to quibble over fine ethical points, succinctly sums up his situation: "I had not failed, I had not died, therefore I had won" (92). Denied their waterskins and equipped only with a knife and flint, Jacobus and his faithful Klawer embark on an existence far more primitive than that of Cruso and Friday in *Foe*. Jacobus adapts readily to the "Bushman" life; he fashions a willow bow and, with arrows dipped in herbal poison, brings down a buck; in leaner times they subsist on roots and nestlings. Klawer, ironically, is less adaptable and soon falls ill, because, Jacobus believes, he lacks a spirited will and has the "constitution of a slave" (94). Unable to move, Klawer urges his master to proceed without him, which Jacobus does, falsely promising to return.

Traveling alone and exultant "like a young man whose mother has just died" (95), Jacobus resumes the psychic metamorphosis that he had begun during his illness. In a state of euphoria, free to "initiate" himself into the desert life, he yodels, growls, hisses, screams, dances, and spins. He links himself to the earth, kicks, hugs, and claws it; he even bores a hole to copulate with it—which he calls the "ur-act"—but laughter and joy reduce his penis to a "four-inch dangle" (95). He shouts, "God, God, God, why do you love me so? . . . I love you too, God. I love everything. I love the stones and the sand and the bushes and the sky and Klawer and those others and every worm, every fly in the world" (95). But he asks that God not let anything return his love, for he wants to be alone, like the stones, which he loves best, "so introverted, so occupied quietly in being" (96). Finally, he identifies with an intrepid black beetle who will try every route of escape until captured, and then will feign death so resolutely that it will not flinch even if its legs are pulled off one by one. This creature he associates with the founder of stoicism, Zeno, and with the dichotomy paradox: "Now I am only halfway dead. . . . Now I am only seven-eighths dead. . . . Now I am only fifteen-sixteenths dead" ad infinitum (96). In his captivity under the Hottentots, he believes that he followed the example of the Zeno beetle, prepared to lose "metaphoric legs," hiding himself away in the "blindest alley of the labyrinth of myself" (96).

Jacobus, Narcissus-like, longs for a reflecting pool in which to see himself. With unconscious irony, he ponders the nature of savagery, and wonders whether or not the Namaqua and Hottentots qualify as savages. Failing to see his own reflection, he defines true savagery as "a way of life based on disdain for the value of human life and a sensual delight in the pain of others" (a personality type that Coetzee explores

in depth in Colonel Joll of *Waiting for the Barbarians*). Jacobus concludes
that the Namaqua are not true savages: "Even I know more about savagery than they" (98). As though to demonstrate the point, he strides
across three hundred miles of desert clad in his "glorious manhood"
and in the only remaining vestige of his civilized garb, his shoes. Upon
reaching the edge of his settlement, he knifes a docile cow and plants
an arrow in the thigh of the herder, enjoying a "day of bloodlust and
anarchy . . . an assault on colonial property" (106). As his final act
before returning home, he enacts a ritual sacrifice, like "God in a whirl-
wind," and slits the throat of one of the symbols for Christ, a lamb, "an
innocent little fellow," and strides through the door bearing the liver,
his "favorite cut" (100), on 12 October 1760.

Peter Knox-Shaw gives an insightful reading of Jacobus's psychic
journey:

In the brilliance of the desert the narrator confronts—in place of a dark, infinitely recessive self—a center of complete emptiness. The lack of an apparent
self prompts him to view his identity as coterminous with that of the external
world, "I am all that I see" (p. 84); but in doing so he involves the entire universe in his sense of nullity, his inner death. Hence his need for violence. For
only by demonstrating his separateness—only by bringing death into the world—
can he preserve a belief in external life.[19]

Heart of Darkness

Jacobus's brief final narrative is a vivid enactment of his earlier reflection "entombed in its coffer my heart too had lived in darkness all
its life" (78). Entitled "Second journey to the land of the Great Namaqua [Expedition of Captain Hendrik Hop, 16 August 1761–27 April
1762]," this narrative depicts Jacobus's wrathful punishment of his hu-
miliators. He wastes no time on preliminaries. The tale opens with his
first kill, a "girl, a pretty child on the way to the stream." After placing
a shot neatly between her shoulder-blades, he addresses his most durable deity: "I will not fail you, beautiful death" (100). Upon locating his
four unfaithful servants, he enacts his own definition of savagery, dis-
daining human life and taking a sensual delight in the pain of others.
Like a cat with doomed mice, he prolongs his pleasure, first making "a
brief sermon" in Dutch. The salient points (incomprehensible to his
trembling victims) are three: (1) we do not require that God be good,
only that he "never forget us" (as the servants had forgotten Jacobus);
(2) the sparrow will fall (as they will fall), but with design; "the sparrow
is cheap but he is not forgotten"; (3) acts of justice and injustice "all
bear their place in the economy of the whole" (101), a sentiment that
would have pleased Alexander Pope. By way of a benediction, he pro-
nounces upon his parishioners the sentence of death.

Jacobus is not without self-awareness in these acts. In a philosophical leap linking stoicism with existentialism, he reflects: "My despair was despair at the undifferentiated plenum, which is after all nothing but the void dressed up as being" (101). More self-critically, "I was undergoing nothing less than a failure of the imagination before the void. I was sick at heart" (102). Nonetheless, these thoughts are followed by prolonged executions, the rape of a child by a Griqua, and a general torching of the village. Whereas the violence in "The Vietnam Project" was largely distant, abstract, filtered through Eugene Dawn's imagination, Coetzee makes the slaughter here concrete, inescapable. As Knox-Shaw observes: "Nothing offsets the sadistic agency of the narrator: in so far as the suffering of Coetzee's victims is recorded, it is through the gloating eye of their killer" ("*Dusklands,*" 73).

His revenge and blood-lust sated, Jacobus has afterthoughts. In a Blakean reflection, he wonders if he may have slaughtered "an immense world of delight closed off to my senses? May I not have killed something of inestimable value?" (106). He quickly rejects this possibility, arguing to himself that if the Hottentots are a world of delight, it is an "impenetrable world" to men like himself. In any case, he reasons, after his expulsion from the village, he became a "pallid symbol": his revenge reasserted his reality. Moreover (as though arguing Camus' idea that we all have "plague"), he sees his deeds as a sacrifice for his countrymen, committing upon the Hottentot "the murders we all have wished. All are guilty, without exception" (106). Does Jacobus fear his own death? Possibly yes, probably no: "A world without me is inconceivable" (107). Beneath this veneer of egotism can be seen the substance of a man without a sense of self, seeking his being through the annihilation of the Other. Jonathan Crewe notes that the two parts of *Dusklands* present "the lands of the West, of 'civilization's' twilight. America, South Africa: 'voids' into which the Western consciousness, bearing its philosophical freight, first explodes, and then, confronting both finitude and nothingness . . . implodes in psychotic rage" ("*Dusklands,*" 92–93).

History, Fiction, and Fabrication

In our interview, Coetzee pointed out that in his fictive narrative framework, he is supposed to appear only as a translator, "Which of course is a lie," and that his father is actually a retired attorney, not the "late Dr. S. J. Coetzee" who is supposed to have presented lectures on pioneer Afrikaners at the University of Stellenbosch between 1934 and 1948. J. M. Coetzee further remarked (quoted in part earlier): "That's the false historical link that has been inserted. It all simply has to do with my conception of the way in which the founding fathers of the

South African state have run the history of the country since the seventeenth century." A footnote to this narrative spoofery is that the thanks that the author gives in his preface to "Dr. P.K.E. van Joggum and Mrs. M. J. Potgieter" is approximate Afrikaans for thanks to Dr. Baboon (*joggom*) and Mrs. Potfoundry (*pot-gietery*).

The face of an ironic J. M. Coetzee is barely concealed by the mask of "Dr. S. J. Coetzee's" Afterword. The good doctor sees Jacobus Coetzee (the Christian connotations of S. J. and J. C. become a travesty) as one of the first South African heroes, "honorable if minor," and S. J.'s own writing about Jacobus, incongruously, as "a work of piety but also a work of history" (108). After noting the variant spellings of the surname (Coetzee, Coetsee, Coetse), he praises Jacobus's legitimate accomplishments: he was one of the first Afrikaners to cross the Orange River and sight the giraffe; he was also an outstanding producer of skins and ivory tusks, generating large profits for the Company (linking him with Conrad's Kurtz).

Much of the rest of the doctor's description is a model of unconscious ironic romanticizing. Jacobus is seen dropping from his saddle, "first the right foot, then the left . . . the cobalt smoke from the muzzle of his gun perhaps by now wholly mingled with the lighter blue of the sky" (110). He is an "humble man who did not play God, is unlikely to have tortured his animals" (111) (there is no mention of his torturing Hottentots). Contrarily, "Coetzee rode like a god through a world only partly named, differentiating and bringing into existence" (116).

Dr. S. J.'s version of the relation of Jacobus and other Afrikaners with the Bushmen and Hottentots is revisionary history. He records that Bushmen were known to mutilate cattle (113) and disembowel their enemies (119). Since captured Bushmen women and children usually made excellent slaves, the Afrikaners' slaughter of the adult male was "thus in no sense genocidal. Even some adult males survived in captivity" (114). The Hottentots, "a debased people" (117), did experience a kind of cultural genocide in that their "language has perished" (115). This is just as well, for they fare badly in comparison with the Namaqua, a people "of great interest, of great piquancy," as evidenced in part by Namaqua laws and punishments: "for stock theft a bath of hot resin, for incest loss of limb, for homicide the clubbing out of the brains" (118). As for the Hottentots and Bushmen, they are recompensed for their losses by having learned "the lesson of the Fall: one cannot live forever in Eden. The Company's men were only playing the part of the angel with the flaming sword" (110). (One wonders who played the part of the serpent in S. J.'s revision of the Eden myth.) Finally, he is indeed thankful that "the exercise of cultural influence" was wholly by Europeans upon the Hottentots, deftly ignoring Jacobus's manic savagery in the wilderness. Similarly, the doctor remains silent about the Great Explorer's murderous second expedition, for it is "an historical irrelevance"; only man's "thrust into the future is history" (121).

Dr. S. J.'s purblind chronicling of the devastating effect of Europeans on South African culture and society evidences that he shares the inhumanity, but not the candor, of his hero Jacobus. More importantly, it illuminates the significance of the quotation from Flaubert that J. M. Coetzee chose as the epigraph for "The Narrative of Jacobus Coetzee": "What is important is the philosophy of history." As Coetzee stated in our interview, and as he has demonstrated through his character S. J., "history is time on which meaning has been imposed, which we call historical meaning, so that time is not just one thing after another, or one event after another. It is time and event that seem to be moving in a direction." For S. J. and Jacobus, the "direction" in which history is moving is clearly the subjection of African people to the mastery of European rule.

While Coetzee is using fiction to reflect a philosophy of history, his fiction is not without historical basis. Peter Knox-Shaw has demonstrated that Coetzee made use of *The Journals of Brink and Rhenius* (1761– 62), the *Travels* (1780–85) of Le Vaillant, John Barrow's *Travels* (1801), as well as other items listed in S. J.'s *Notes* (*Dusklands*, 122), to establish the historical authenticity that he would then undermine with fictional reflexivity ("*Dusklands*," 65–81). As Knox-Shaw observes: "Not perhaps since Defoe has fiction so effectively assumed a specious armor of document" (74), and yet that documentation is an "ironic mask to what is essentially an anti-documentary polemic" (66).

In the second part of *Dusklands* we are given four documents: (1) the "Translator's Preface" by a fictive "J. M. Coetzee"; (2) "The Narrative of Jacobus Coetzee"; (3) the "Afterword" of S. J. Coetzee, who is presented as J. M.'s "father"; and (4) the "Appendix: Deposition of Jacobus Coetzee (1760)." The "Narrative" is the main text of the *nouvelle* and is supposed to have been published in the original Dutch in 1951 by S. J. under the title *Het relaas Jacobus Coetzee, Janszoon* [son of John]. J. M. Coetzee claims to have "translated" into English the *Relaas* and the Appendix from the original Dutch and S. J.'s Afterword from Afrikaans. Jacobus's Appendix deposition is the *nouvelle*'s only authentic historical document, which the illiterate Jacobus reported orally on 18 November 1760, concerning his first journey among the Namaquas. Jacobus related his deposition to an O. M. Bergh, "Councillor & Secretary of the Castle of Good Hope," who recorded the report. S. J. regards Berg's transcription as the work of "a Castle hack" who wrote down Jacobus's story with the "impatience of a bureaucrat" (perhaps a Kafkaesque allusion by a covert J. M.), a bureaucrat whose principal

concern was the commercial interest of the Company. Thus, the Deposition emphasizes Jacobus's reports of wild game, mineral ore depos-
its, timberlands, and the potential of various tribes as suppliers of goods.

There is, however, one puzzling curiosity: Jacobus's report of the
Namaqua's story of an eloquent people called Damroquas, "of a tawny
or yellow appearance with long heads of hair and linen clothes," who
dwell about twenty days' journey north of the Great Namaquas. S. J.
regards the story as a Namaqua "fable" which the too credulous Jacobus brought back and which the "Castle hack" recorded for its possible
commercial value. The problem, however, is that Jacobus makes no
reference in his narrative to any story of exotic long-haired people to
the North, an odd omission for such a colorful tale teller. S. J., apparently unwittingly, provides a clue to this puzzle when he notes that the
story of the long-hairs "led to the dispatch of Hendrik Hop's fruitless
expedition of 1761–62" (109). The solution seems to be that Jacobus
Coetzee, a fictional-historical figure created by J. M. Coetzee, and published by J. M.'s fictional father, S. J. Coetzee, has created his own fiction of the long-haired people in order to persuade the Castle to un-
derwrite his second journey, wherein he covertly planned to take revenge
on his betrayers.

A much more elaborate example of fiction evolving from "history"
occurs within the Afterword of S. J., who usually limits himself to biased
historical reporting. However, toward the end of his essay, he expresses
a wish that his primary documents contained more colorful material:
"Hunting adventures lend excitement, however spurious, to history"
(116). Apparently dazzled by the idea, he launches into a fabrication in
which the great white hunter, Jacobus, takes off his trousers, "as is the
wont of elephant hunters," and shoots "a bull stone dead with a ball
behind the shoulder." Jacobus then kills an elephant cow with a single
shot behind the ear, after which the hunters enjoy a meal of elephant
heart, "a notable delicacy." S. J. concludes this "historical" vignette with
an odd address to the reader: "I trust you have enjoyed this adventure"
(117).

Having launched himself from history into fiction, S. J. proceeds with
another tale, this time in the documentary detailed cataloguing style of
the "Ithaca" chapter of Joyce's *Ulysses*. After Jacobus and his party have
traversed a frozen pass in the Khamies mountains, S. J. becomes a kind
of time-traveling sleuth, documenting the relics of their passage:

At one of their halts (August 18) the expedition left behind: the ashes of the
night fire, combustion complete, a feature of dry climates; faeces dotted in
mounds over a broad area . . . urine stains with minute traces of copper salts;
tea leaves . . . five inches of braided oxhide rope; tobacco ash; and a musket
ball. The faeces dried in the course of a day. Rope and bones were eaten by a

hyena on August 22. A storm on November 2 scattered all else. The musket
ball was not there on August 18, 1933. (118–19)

The effect of this, of course, is to shatter the illusion of historicity. J. M.
Coetzee forces us to remember that we are reading *his* creation, and
that in the realm of fiction, the imagination reigns.

There are also examples of self-conscious narration in the main body
of Jacobus's text. At the beginning of the "Second Journey," just after
he has killed the "pretty child" on the outskirts of the Namaqua village,
Coetzee's Jacobus employs a device that Nabokov has used rather often,
directly asking the reader to complete the details of the author's "stage
setting." Jacobus excuses himself from the task, saying, "Fill in the
morning smoke rising straight in the air, the first flies making for the
corpse, and you have the tableau" (100). Another artifice which Coetzee uses extensively in *In the Heart of the Country* and in the conclusion
of *Foe* makes its first appearance in *Dusklands:* the twice-told tale, in
which the narrator convincingly describes an event, then retells the episode, significantly altering its substance. During the long trek back from
the Namaquas, Jacobus describes a scene in which he and Klawer are
attempting to ford the swollen waters of the Great River. Klawer is in
the lead, testing the bottom. Suddenly, Jacobus tells us, the "violence
of the current . . . swept Klawer over the shallows into deep water.
With horror I watched my faithful servant . . . until he disappeared
from sight around a bend and went to his death" (94). In the next
paragraph, without a blush, Jacobus retells the crossing from the beginning: "We had to probe the bottom before each step. . . . But sodden
and shivering we finally reached the south bank" (94). The purpose of
such counterfeiting can only be to remind the reader that the adventure he is experiencing is solely controlled by the narrator, and that
behind the mind of Jacobus is another consciousness, that of J. M.
Coetzee.

There are other examples of fictive reflexivity. In his initial encounter with the Namaqua, Jacobus summarizes for the reader his pro forma
greeting, one we might expect from a commercial explorer: "We came
in peace. We brought gifts and promises of friendship. We were simple
hunters. . . . Travellers had spoken of the hospitality and generosity
of the great Namaqua people" (66). Quite different is the interior
monologue Jacobus has just before his spoken greeting:

the inner debate (resist? submit?), underlings rolling their eyeballs . . . words
of greeting, firm tones, Peace! Tobacco! . . . the feast, glut, nightfall, murder
foiled . . . the inner debate . . . the shot . . . the pursuing horde, the race
for the river . . . the inner debate . . . ritual dismemberment . . . limbs to
the dogs, privates to the first wife . . . the inner debate, the cowardly blow

. . . escape, night chase . . . darkness at noon, victory . . . return to civilization.(65–66)

Jacobus's use of anaphora and his stream of consciousness reckoning
of the myriad possibilities awaiting him tells us about his anxieties and
aspirations and at the same time reminds us that if this is an eighteenth-century narrative, James Joyce was born much earlier than we
supposed.

Coetzee's accomplishments in his first published work of fiction are
considerable. He has produced a formally complex work combining
contemporary American politics and eighteenth-century South African
history with skillfully rendered psychological realism and self-reflexive
fictional techniques. On the other hand, the two *nouvelles* do not really
merge as one work, despite their shared themes. Additionally, "Vietnam" suffers from a certain narrative aridity and lack of sense of place,
in contrast to the robust and tangible tale Jacobus tells.

Knox-Shaw has expressed another reservation, noted earlier: "It is
regrettable that a writer of such considerable and varied talents should
play down the political and economic aspects of history in favor of a
psychopathology of Western life" (*"Dusklands,"* 79). Earlier in the same
essay, Knox-Shaw seems to have answered his objection, at least in part,
when he points out that "indeed it is essential to John Coetzee's purposes in *Dusklands* that his explorer should emerge as a representative
figure not only in the context of Afrikanerdom but of Western culture
as well" (76). Coetzee is ultimately pursuing the metaphysical basis of
Western consciousness, not economics or politics, which in any case are
to some degree manifestations of psychological and metaphysical forces.
As Wood notes, Coetzee presents "not simply a case study of a causality
of the Colonial inheritance, but more broadly and fundamentally
speaking, of the Cartesian inheritance" (*"Dusklands,"* 21).

In the same vein, Stephen Watson asked Coetzee about a common
theme in *Dusklands* and *In the Heart of the Country:* the "psychology of
power" in lands where "everything is permissible" which "prevents that
relation between men out of which reality is composed." Coetzee responded, "I think that the situation in both books is the situation which
you describe—of living among people without reciprocity, so that there
is only an 'I' and the 'You' is not on the same basis, the 'You' is a
debased 'You' " (*Speak,* 23). As we shall see, Magda of *In the Heart of the
Country,* like Dawn and Jacobus, is unable to transcend the Cartesian
duality of I and Other, although she struggles to achieve that transcendence through means never imagined by the protagonists of *Dusklands.*

NOTES

1. J. M. Coetzee in interview with Stephen Watson, *Speak* 1, no. 3 (1978):23;
in interview with Folke Rhedin, *Kunapipi* 6, no. 1 (1984):9.

2. W.J.B. Wood, "*Dusklands* and 'The Impregnable Stronghold of the Intellect,'" *Theoria* (1980): 14.

3. Jonathan Crewe, "*Dusklands,*" *Contrast* 9, no. 11 (1974): 90.

4. Stephen Watson, "Colonialism in the Novels of J. M. Coetzee," *Research in African Literatures* 17 (1986): 371.

5. Sarah Christie, Geoffrey Hutchings, and Don Maclennan, eds., *Perspectives on South African Fiction* (Johannesburg: Ad. Donker, 1980), 182.

6. J. M. Coetzee, "How I Learned About America—and Africa—in Texas," *New York Times Book Review,* 9 April 1984, 9.

7. J. M. Coetzee, quoted in "Lifting Coetzee's Veil," *World Press Review* 32, no. 7 (July 1985): 60.

8. Fyodor Dostoevsky, *Notes from Underground,* translated with an introduction by Ralph Matlaw (New York: Dutton, 1960), 3.

9. Edward Wasiolek, *Dostoevsky: The Major Fiction* (Cambridge: M.I.T. Press, 1964) 39–59; Monroe C. Beardsley, "Dostoevsky's Metaphor of the Underground," *Journal of the History of Ideas* 3 (June 1942): 265–90.

10. J. M. Coetzee, "Confession and Double Thoughts: Tolstoy, Rousseau, Dostoevsky," *Comparative Literature* 37, no. 3 (Summer 1985): 220.

11. Graham Greene, *The Power and the Glory* (New York: Bantam, 1968), 123.

12. Jan Haluska, "Master and Slave in the First Four Novels of J. M. Coetzee" (Ph.D. diss., University of Tennessee, 1987), 23.

13. Michael Vaughan, "Literature and Politics: Currents in South African Writing in the Seventies," *Journal of Southern African Studies* 9, no. 1 (1982): 122–23.

14. Christie, et al., eds., *Perspectives,* 178.

15. *Encyclopedia of South Africa.* 5th ed. (London: Frederick Warne & Co., 1970), 118.

16. J. M. Coetzee, "The White Tribe," *Vogue* (March 1986): 491.

17. Teresa Dovey, *The Novels of J. M. Coetzee: Lacanian Allegories,* Human Sciences Research Council Publication Series, no. 86 (Johannesburg: Ad. Donker, 1988), 88.

18. Samuel Beckett, *First Love and Other Stories* (New York: Grove, 1974), 20.

19. Peter Knox-Shaw, "*Dusklands:* A Metaphysics of Violence," *Commonwealth Novel in English* 14, no. 1 (1983):78.

4

In the Heart of the Country:
The Subversion of an
African Farm

PSYCHOLOGICAL REALISM:
THE INDETERMINATE NARRATIVE

In the Heart of the Country was first published in an English language edition in Great Britain by Secker and Warburg in 1977; the first South African edition, in English with the dialogue in Afrikaans, appeared under the Ravan imprint in 1978. Coetzee translated the Afrikaans for the English language editions. As noted, this second novel received South Africa's most prestigious literary award, the CNA Prize, and strong praise from some critics, most notably, Stephen Watson and Joan Gillmer. With specific reference to *In the Heart of the Country,* Watson contends that " 'all of Europe' (and North America) has gone into the making of Coetzee—or at least into the making of his books. He has produced by far the most intellectual and indeed intellectualizing fiction of any South African or African writer."[1] Gillmer sees this second novel as "arguably the best of Coetzee's [first] three works of fiction," citing its "emotional intensity" as well as "the tight control of the language."[2]

The book has prompted some negative reactions as well, primarily from those demanding a more aggressive political stance from the author. Roland Smith, curiously, insinuates that Coetzee adopted a first-person narrative in order to avoid being held responsible for the novel's political implications: "They are reflections made by the protagonist and therefore cannot be attributed to the author. . . . "[3] As noted earlier, Michael Vaughan also presents an ad hominem attack: "He is a Coetzee among Coetzees. He too is the subject of an ascribed mode of consciousness, that very one proper to the Northern European Protestant type of colonizer-enslaver of his fiction."[4]

The implication that Coetzee does not wish to be associated with the political import of his fiction is certainly strange, given his forthright opposition in both speech and writing to the policies of the South African Nationalist party.[5] In our interview in 1984, Coetzee took such attacks in stride, saying of the reception of his novels: "Back in South Africa there is another type of framework in which they are read, which is very heavily influenced by Marxism, by general Third World thinking. . . . The primary question is, 'Where does this fit into the political struggle?' "

In the Heart of the Country, is, like the two *nouvelles* of *Dusklands,* an extended interior monologue, consisting of 266 numbered entries in diary form, although it is not specified that the entries comprise a diary. The narrator is Magda, a repressed, introverted, perhaps insane spinster of indeterminate age. She lives at about the turn of the century[6] in virtual seclusion on a remote sheep farm with her widowed father, whom she regards, at times, as a domineering martinet, the archetypal Afrikaner *Voortrekker* (pioneer). The indeterminate, contradictory, self-reflexive narrative that Coetzee used occasionally with Jacobus predominates here. Indeed it is impossible to ascertain whether any of the events Magda describes happen anywhere but in her mind. Coetzee remarked in the introduction to his reading from *In the Heart of the Country* in Lexington in 1984, "In the course of the action people get killed or raped, but perhaps not really, perhaps only in the overactive imagination of the story teller."

What *seems* to happen, briefly, is that Magda, out of resentment and jealousy over a liaison she believes her father has established with their brown-skinned servant, Klein-Anna, murders her father twice—once in her imagination, once perhaps actually. Magda then tries to establish a position of mastery over Klein-Anna and her husband Hendrik, and fails. She next tries to develop a relationship of equality with them, and fails again. Hendrik, she believes, rapes her, after which he and his wife abandon the farm. At the novel's end, Magda is left utterly alone, talking with the corpse of her dead father and trying to make sense of her experience by communing with "sky-gods," whom she believes fly overhead and send her messages in a strange language.

All of Magda's narrative is clouded with uncertainty. This indeterminacy is evident from the opening sentences, in which Magda presents herself as an observer of her father bringing home his new bride (who, we later surmise, exists only in Magda's imagination). The "newlyweds" are "in a dog-cart drawn by a horse with an ostrich-plume." This is quickly modified: "Or perhaps they were drawn by two plumed donkeys, that also is possible"; then the scene is repudiated altogether: "More detail I cannot give unless I begin to embroider, for I was not watching" (1). Thus, the reader is bewildered from the outset.

During the writer's workshop which Coetzee conducted in Lexington in 1984, I asked him to comment on the unreliable narrator of *In the Heart of the Country*. He replied:

That's another game, where . . . how shall I put it? When you opt for a single point of view from inside a single character, you can be opting for psychological realism, a depiction of one person's inner consciousness. And the word I stress there is realism, psychological realism. And I suppose that what is going on in *In the Heart of the Country* is that that kind of realism is being subverted because, you know, she kills her father, and her father comes back, and she kills him again, then the book goes on for a bit, and then he's there again. So that's a different kind of game, an anti-realistic kind of game.

Coetzee's subversion of the realistic mode has been the subject of some critical discussion. When Stephen Watson interviewed Coetzee in 1978, Watson pointed out that it was implausible that an eighteenth-century frontiersman like Jacobus should present complex, modern meditations on the metaphysics of being, and that Magda, a colonial spinster, should speak in a manner that is obviously associated with twentieth-century urban consciousness. The following exchange took place:

Coetzee: I would reply to a criticism like that by saying that (a) Jacobus Coetzee is not an 18th century frontiersman and (b) Magda is not a colonial spinster.

Watson: Who are they then?

Coetzee: I . . . figures in books.[7]

Eight years later when Watson published his essay on colonialism in Coetzee's fiction, he had carefully thought through Coetzee's deconstruction of realism, noting that the first three novels all conflate historical periods "with a seeming disregard for all historical veracity," and that Magda's thoughts betray not only an "urban" consciousness, but a familiarity with French surrealism as well as structuralist linguistic theory ("Colonialism," 372–73). Watson concluded: "*In the Heart of the Country* is, on one level, concerned to demonstrate that realism is not real at all, but simply a production of language, a code that people have come to accept as 'natural.' Coetzee wants to create what Barthes would have called a 'writeable' text . . . one which does not attempt to reduce the potentially multiple meanings, the 'plurality' of the text, by fixing one single meaning for it" (373–74). Vaughan adds that by dividing the novel into numbered paragraphs, Coetzee alludes "to the artificiality of fictional progressions. There is no unequivocal progression in Magda's monologue" ("Literature and Politics," 125).

Readers have also seen *In the Heart of the Country* as a deconstruction of the pastoral mode—and not surprisingly. A work which presents life on the farm in terms of incestual desire, patricide, interracial rape, and insanity can hardly be construed as carrying on the South African pastoral tradition. Dovey sees *In the Heart of the Country* as a "re-writing" and a "deliberate parody of [Olive] Schreiner's literary enterprise"[8] in *The Story of an African Farm* (despite the sense of absence and emptiness Schreiner conveys), since Coetzee's work "simultaneously recuperates and subverts its origins in the tradition" of the pastoral mode (192). Paul Rich carries this idea further, describing the work as an " 'anti-pastoral' novel in that it takes an idealized rural situation, in the Borgesian sense, and subjects it to a merciless scrutiny in order to try and reveal some inner truth about the nature of real social reality."[9]

Coetzee's perception of the reality of South African society and culture is bleak. In an interview published shortly after the appearance of *In the Heart of the Country*, he commented on the implications of the desert setting of the novel:

the desert archetype is about a lack of society and the lack of a shared culture, a feeling of anomie, a feeling of solitariness, a feeling of not having human ties with the people around one. . . . We find ourselves living in a country of fragmented or obsolete cultures: African culture is fragmented, Afrikaner rural culture is equally fragmented, and the cities are just agglomerations, with no distinctive urban culture. So for the people whose roots have been cut, who have no sense of identity to the extent of not even knowing what their roots were, the image of the desert in which one is solitary has a lot of meaning, and yes, I would say that socially it has a lot of relevance. (*Speak*, 22)

Beasts in the Labyrinth: Life with Father

Magda is a living embodiment of the isolation, fragmentation, and anomie Coetzee describes. Her mind becomes a labyrinth, and the reader is invited to play Ariadne to his or her own Theseus: play out the thread through any number of passages in the labyrinth, so long as you find your way back from the Minotaur, the "beast" which Magda believes "stalks" her.

The identity of this "beast" is not immediately clear. Perhaps it is the stern father, "stiff as a ramrod" (31), and his voluptuous young nonexistent "bride," who licks "sweet mutton fat from her lips" (1) and displaces Magda. Or it may be the brown-skinned servant couple who work on the farm, Klein-Anna (Afrikaans, petite Anna), with her "sly doe eyes, her narrow hips" (26), who becomes the master's mistress and also displaces Magda; or Hendrik, Klein-Anna's husband, "a fine chest, strong lungs, a man" (104), the obedient—"Yes my baas. Thank you, my baas" (20)—servant-in-rebellion who apparently rapes Magda. Or perhaps the beast is Magda herself, "the grim widow-daughter of the dark father" (3). In her monologue, Magda ponders the identity of the Minotaur;

> But the beast is not enchanted by my prattle. From hour to hour he stalks me through the afternoon. I hear his velvet pad, smell his fetid breath. . . . Somewhere on the farm my father roams, burning with shame. . . . Is my father the beast? Elsewhere on the farm loom Hendrik and Anna. . . . Is Hendrik the beast, the insulted husband, the serf trodden under his master's boot, rising to roar for vengeance? Anna, with her sharp little teeth, her hot armpits—is she the beast, the woman subtle, lascivious, insatiable? . . .
>
> Who is the beast among us? . . . I must ask: Is it my own snarl I hear in the undergrowth? Am I the one to fear, ravening, immoderate, because here in the heart of the country where space radiates out from me to all the four corners of the earth there is nothing that can stop me? As I sit quietly gazing at my roses waiting for the afternoon to end I find that hard to accept. (49–50)

Magda's thoughts lead us to three aspects of the labyrinth: the father as "beast"; the master/slave relationships of the father, Magda, Hendrik, and Anna; and, finally, the key role that language plays in these relationships.

Magda's feelings toward her father are a composite of contradictions: fear, resentment, desire, admiration, murderous rage, and, following his death, affectionate companionship. One of her most vivid descriptions conveys her perception of her father's frightening, domineering nature:

> The boots, the thud of the boots, the black brow, the black eyeholes, the black hole of the mouth from which roars the great NO, iron cold, thunderous, that blasts me and buries me and locks me up. . . . I squirm, again the boot is raised over me, the mouthhole opens, and the great wind blows, chilling me to my pulpy heart. (51)

There are moments in the novel when this description seems appropriate, and there are others when it seems a preposterous exaggeration.

Early in the novel Magda states that there are many "melancholy spinsters" like herself, victims of the "childhood rape": "Wooed when we were little by our masterful fathers, we are bitter vestals, spoiled for life" (3). While she labels this "fancy," she insists that there is a "kernel of truth" in it. From the context of the novel it seems clear that the "rape" refers to the dominance/submission roles played out by father and daughter, respectively. Throughout, we see Magda drawing her father's bath, preparing his meals, cutting his hair, taking off his boots, a "drudgemaiden" (32), as she refers to herself. At the same time, she has incestuous desires for her father, not surprisingly, given their isolated existence "in a district outside the law, where the bar against incest is often down" (138). She reflects, "when I think of male flesh, white, heavy, dumb, whose flesh can it be but his?" (9). She has a nightmare fantasy in which she gives birth to the "son of the father, Antichrist of the desert . . . an epileptic Fuhrer" (10) who leads a band of Hottentots to their slaughter and mass burial. Magda reflects, "Laboring under my father's weight I struggle to give life to a world but seem to engender only death" (10). She has thoughts about his penis; in her fantasied murder of her father and her imaginary step-mother, Magda perceives her father's "tired blind fish, cause of all my woe, lolling in his groin (would that it had been dragged out long ago with all its roots and bulbs!)" (11). Following what appears to be the actual shooting of her father, she sees him naked and has some whimsical thoughts: "The sex is smaller than I thought it would be . . . a pale boy, a midget, a dwarf, an idiot son" who has been hidden away in the cellar "talking to the spiders," is one night given new clothes, set free, "pampered, feasted, and then executed. Poor little thing" (69). Obviously, whatever incestuous eroticism is contained here is entangled with violent hatred and childlike curiosity.

Her barely submerged anger at her father is oddly counterpointed at other times by Magda's admiration and sympathy for the man. In words that seem drawn from some cinema of the Old West, or S. J. Coetzee's romanticized conception of Jacobus, she describes his daily return: "he comes home nevertheless in pride and glory, a fine figure of a man . . . riding in every evening against a flaming sky as though he had spent the whole day waiting for this moment, his horse tethered in a thorn-tree's shade just over the rise" (31). In a rare moment of compassion, Magda attempts to excuse her father's darker side: "He hates only because he dare not love. He hates in order to hold himself together. He is not a bad man, despite all. He is not unjust" (52). Indeed, this appears to be borne out in the one scene where Magda seems to report the speech and movements of her father directly rather than at some remove through the filter of her consciousness. Angered that her father is in bed with the servant Klein-Anna, Magda fires one rifle shot through his bedroom window; with her eyes closed, she fires another round just as her father grabs the barrel of the gun, and he is shot. Slumped against the footboard of the bed, a hole in his belly the size of her thumb and a gaping hole in his back, surrounded by blood and flies, he hardly sounds like a tyrant: " 'Fetch Hendrik,' he says, 'Tell Hendrik to come, please' " (65). He asks her to please bring some

brandy, the doctor, something for the pain, and in all of this does not
blame or judge her.

A key to the relationship between this enigmatic father and his paradoxical daughter may be contained in two rather cryptic passages. One
is a dream Magda has about a bush that "glows with an unearthly light"
and sheds its radiance on her: "There is a scheme of interpretation, I
am sure, according to which my dream about the bush is a dream about
my father. But who is to say what a dream about my father is?" (73).
Assuming that this enticement draws us toward a comparison of Moses
seeing the angel of God in the burning bush that "was not consumed"
(Exod. 3:2), we might say that the dream is about those aspects of her
father that can be associated with the God of the Old Testament: au-
thoritarian, judgmental, retributive. This is the father that Magda feels
compelled to bow down to and whom she simultaneously wishes to destroy.

In contrast, the second passage depicts an odd union between father
and daughter, the entwinement of Magda's and her father's feces after
she and her father have taken their turns on the bucket-latrine outside
the house. His feces emit a "hellish gust, bloody feral, the kind that
flies love best" while hers are "dark, olive with bile, hard-packed, kept
in too long, old, tired." After Hendrik empties their common bucket,
"there is a pit where, looped in each other's coils, the father's red snake
and the daughter's black embrace and sleep and dissolve" (32). This is
less Swiftian scatology than a rendering in the most earthy imagery of
Magda's ultimate desire to merge with her father and others, "to be at
home in the world as the meanest beast is at home" (135); to embrace,
and end her solitariness, then to "sleep and dissolve." Despite the agen-
cies of the burning bush and entwined excrement, Magda is left torn
between feelings of hatred and love for her father, and for the society
which he represents.

Allegorical Apartheid

The enigmatic and paradoxical nature of this narrative has given rise
to some interesting critical responses. More than any of Coetzee's other
novels, *In the Heart of the Country* has prompted readings in which the
characters and events are seen as an allegory of modern South Africa.
This is doubtless a consequence of Coetzee's combining thought that is
clearly contemporary with a turn-of-the-century South African setting.
Sheila Roberts, for example, observes that the "splintered, contradictory, miserable" Magda reflects the fragmented consciousness of South
Africa.[10] Roberts interprets the stone farm as "South Africa itself, the
father as the Afrikaner *baas,* and Magda as the ineffectual, dreaming

liberal" (30). Robert Post makes the same connections with the farm but sees the father as "the Afrikaner government," and identifies Magda with the "oppressed black race" in that she, too, is in bondage.[11] In a comparison of the writings of Coetzee and Sheila Fugard, Roland Smith notes that by emphasizing the "psychology of derangement . . . the authors try to make an implicit comment on the present." The protagonists' "bizarre psychological states are paradigms of the bizarre reality in the apartheid state" ("Seventies," 197). André Brink similarly comments that "the tensions at work in apartheid society are internalized into intensely private experience (at the same time attaining the universality of allegory)."[12]

The essence of apartheid society is the continuance of strictly defined roles of dominance and submission. In Coetzee's novel, the master/slave relations are multiple and protean. Magda plays the role of servant/daughter to her father until she rebels and kills him. Hendrik is the archetypal servant to the father and Magda until the murder destroys the social order and Hendrik rebels and apparently rapes Magda, who then becomes subservient to him. Klein-Anna, a woman and a "brown person," remains submissive to the other three principals throughout. One of Magda's earliest self-descriptions underscores the lack of any egalitarian relationships in this society: "I, who living among the downcast have never beheld myself in the equal regard of another's eye, have never held another in the equal regard of mine" (8). She recalls how Hendrik arrived at the farm at the age of sixteen, having come from the village of Armoede (Afrikaans, poverty), seeking work. His hat held humbly in his hand, his speech to the father punctuated by the refrain, "Yes, my baas," he is the essence of the compliant servant. By the end of the novel, however, Magda is aware of the insidious nature of such subservience: "the pitiful warrior in the hills was never as formidable as the enemy who walked in our shadow and said *Yes baas*. To the slave who would only say *Yes* my father could only say *No*, and I after him, and that was the start of all my woe" (129).

These shifting relationships of dominance and submission take us back to Magda's earlier vision of the "beast" which stalks her. She asked, "Is my father the beast?" and then, are the servants, or am I myself the beast? Shortly before her father dies, she envisions another scene: "brother and sister, wife and daughter and concubine prowl and snarl around the bedside listening for the death rattle, or stalk each other through the dim passages of the ancestral home" (70). This passage, and the novel as a whole, strongly suggest that the "beast" is multifaceted, a composite of all of the characters caught in their particular place and time in a labyrinth of master/slave relationships and language.

Breaking the Rules:
Language, Apartheid, and Patricide

In South Africa, as in any society past or present founded on dominance and submission, the continuation of the system is dependent upon the willingness of all the participants to play their roles consistently and to adhere strictly to the rules. In an essay about Afrikaners, Coetzee remarks that he was "born in the twilight of a centuries-old feudal order in which the rights and duties of masters and servants seemed to be a matter of unspoken convention, and in which a mixture of personal intimacy and social distance—a mixture characteristic of societies with a slaveholding past—pervaded all dealings." All that was required was "the iron hand needed to keep the old order running."[13]

What then sunders the social order of this fictional farm, this microcosm of a larger society? It can hardly be the traditional liaison between the white master and the brown-skinned wife of his servant. As Coetzee noted in discussing such relationships in the fiction of South African novelist Sarah Gertrude Millin, the white master "can sleep with black women and father children of mixed blood but cannot give up his sense of racial identity."[14] There is no suggestion that Magda's father gives over his sense of white superiority. He beguiles Klein-Anna with trinkets, candy, and money; she acquiesces to his sexual requests; Hendrik douses his impotent rage with brandy supplied by "the baas" then later vents his fury on his wife through physical and sexual violence. Everyone is playing by the historical rules of the master/slave society.

It is, of course, Magda who ultimately refuses to play by the rules. In her role as spinster/daughter/servant, she is supposed to believe that her father's peccadillos with the servant girl do not exist, or, barring that, that they do not matter. Instead, she sees Klein-Anna as a rival for her father's affection and sexuality, and her father as undermining the very foundation on which the master/servant society is based—hierarchical language:

My father is exchanging forbidden words with Klein-Anna. . . . *We,* he is saying to her, *we two.* . . . There are few enough words true, rock-hard enough to build a life on, and these he is destroying. He believes that he and she can choose their words and make a private language. . . . But there can be no private language. . . . How can I speak to Hendrik as before when they corrupt my speech? How do I speak to them? (35)

In Magda's sociolinguistic formula, the "forbidden words" are societal taboos: "we" between blacks and whites is impossible. The "few words" upon which life is built have to do with the rigid social contract of

South Africa—the restrictive, pragmatic rules of behavior between master and servant. There can be no "private language" between these groups, only the formulaic exchanges which define their social positions.

Magda complains that due to her father's violation of the contract, she cannot speak to the servants "as before," which she describes in an early passage as a semiotic exchange:

I am not spoken to in words, which come to me quaint and veiled, but in signs, in conformations of face and hands, in postures of shoulders and feet, in nuances of tune and tone, in gaps and absences whose grammar has never been recorded. Reading the brown folk I grope, as they grope reading me: for they too hear my words only dully, listening for those overtones of the voice, those subtleties of the eyebrows that tell them my true meaning: "Beware, do not cross me," "What I say does not come from me" (7).

Rather, her communication comes from what her father, and by implication, society, has taught her are the legitimizing bases of their community. It is not surprising that Magda feels that her ontological props have been pulled from under her: "perhaps my rage at my father is simply rage at the violations of the old language, the correct language" (43).

Magda is not the only one to sense that the beginning of the end is at hand. Soon after her father begins his illicit courtship of Klein-Anna, two minor characters, an elderly servant couple who have worked on the farm since Magda's childhood, patriarchal Jacob and his wife *Ou-Anna* (Afrikaans, old/dear-Anna) suddenly leave without explanation (37). In the quiet before the storm, Magda distracts herself with fantasies: for example, a humorous one about her hypothetical marriage to a prototypical country bumpkin, "greedier than most, stupider, uglier, not much of a catch," whom she would have to "guide to the right hole, rendered penetrable with a gob of chickenfat from the pot at the bedside, and endure the huffing and puffing of" (42). Fantasies, however, are no match for sober reality. If Klein-Anna is to be elevated from servitor to seraglio, then perhaps Magda will be forced to adopt a Kafkaesque role: "will I have to come out in the middle of the night like a cockroach to clean up after them?" (53).

In a desperate reversion to childhood, Magda sends urgent appeals through the door that separates her from her father and Klein-Anna, punctuated by the word "Daddy," then intensifies her disruption by ringing the dinner bell outside the door. The reply to her appeal is a blow that leaves her nose bloodied (earlier, her father had gently tried to comfort her). Swelling the action, Magda loads a rifle and fires a shot through her father's bedroom window, "toward the far ceiling of the room." Encouraged by high-pitched screams and "numerous angry lower sounds," she reloads:

I elevate the barrel, close my eyes, and pull the trigger. At the same instant the rifle jerks out of my hands. The detonation is even flatter than before. The whole rifle leaves me, surprisingly. It snakes through the curtains and is gone. I rest on my knees empty-handed. (61)

In both the sexual affair and the patricide, the violation of taboos is ambiguous: the father has apparently had his way with the servant girl, but the nature of the relationship is unclear. Magda wonders at one point if Klein-Anna parts her legs "because he is the master, or are there refinements of pleasure in subjection which wedded love can never give?" (52). On the other hand, Magda later asks Klein-Anna, "What was it like with my father when the two of you spoke? . . . Did he give you good words?" (101–2). If the latter, then the father had flouted the rules of his society and must pay the price. Similarly, in Magda's fantasy "murder" of her father and his new "bride" (11), Magda is subjectively guilty of patricide, but objectively innocent. In the apparent killing of her father, she is objectively guilty (pulling the trigger), but subjectively innocent (seeking attention, firing at the ceiling). In the final analysis, subjective intentions have no more substance than the moving shadows in Plato's cave. Acts count.

Liberal Dreams Lost

By her patricide, Magda has destroyed the old order, but she is powerless to put a new order in its place. In fantasies, she fashions a libertarian dream, in which she and Hendrik (with Klein-Anna assisting) unite to dispose of the body: variously, by sealing off the bedroom, making it a mausoleum (81–82); by detaching the bedroom from the house and floating it off into the night sky (82); and by burning the body on a funeral pyre (82). In her mind, an egalitarian camaraderie emerges: "our labour brings us together . . . I am his equal though I am the weaker. . . . Our honest sweat flows together in the dark warmth" (82). She wishes to whisper to Hendrik, "something kindly and affectionate about Anna" (85). She longs to stroll arm in arm with Anna, "whispering and giggling like a girl," and she surprises herself by inviting the servants to sleep in the house with her: "The words come out without premeditation. I feel joy. That must be how other people speak, from their hearts" (87). For the first time, Magda perceives language as a true medium of exchange, rather than a means of alienating and separating. In a moment of revelation that seems to have been inspired by William Blake, she confides to Anna, "energy is eternal delight . . . my tongue is forked with fire . . . but it has all been turned uselessly inward . . . I have never learned to talk with another person. . . . I have never known words of true exchange, Anna" (101).

If the farm can be taken as a microcosm of South Africa, then Coetzee seems to be projecting that the long-overdue changes in that society will come suddenly and, they will be fraught with continued misunderstanding and violence. One does not overcome lifetime roles in a moment. When Magda kisses her forehead, Anna "stiffens and endures" her. When she implores Anna to call her by her first name, Anna finds it impossible and continues to address her as "Miss" (102). However Magda may fantasize about an egalitarian society, the reality is, that with the patriarchal order dead and the new order powerless to be born, all of these people are directionless. Magda has been a servant to her father as much as the brown folk have; she is accustomed to taking, not giving orders. When Hendrik and Anna wait for her directions, she can think of nothing to tell them (80). Hendrik's rebellion and Magda's prejudice soon surface. When he refuses to help her bury the father (and implicitly, the old order), she snaps, "You damned *hotnot*" (91) (Afrikaans, hottentot, with a pejorative sense of lackey). The economic system also collapses. Never having managed money, Magda has no money to give the servants on the first of the month; Hendrik retaliates by slaughtering a sheep each week. His rebellion becomes blatant when he dresses in her father's best clothes and mocks and leers at her, offering to take off the trousers when Magda objects.

The failure of Magda, Hendrik, and Klein-Anna to offer even the hope of establishing a new order of free individuals demonstrates how *In the Heart of the Country,* like the rest of Coetzee's fiction, breaks with the South African liberal tradition to be found in the works of a writer like Alan Paton and in Nadine Gordimer's earlier fiction. Paul Rich notes that "Coetzee has sought to reveal an inner existential dilemma confronting the inheritors of a European colonial culture that stands without roots or history. At one level, this achievement can be seen to mark a profound break with the previous liberal individualism that has underpinned the South African novel" ("Tradition," 72).

With the exception of Jacobus, who revels in his role of colonial mastery, and Michael K, who chooses to withdraw from the fray, Magda and all of Coetzee's other protagonists are entrapped in hopeless struggles to alter the course of history or to liberate themselves or others from their colonial bonds. Michael Vaughan gives an insightful analysis of this matter, seeing Coetzee's novels as a response to

the patent ineffectuality of liberal ideas and strategies. . . . Liberal aesthetics involves . . . the premise of an ontology of individual freedom, and a consequent belief in the self-correctibility of the (unfree) individual towards free-

dom. . . . Coetzee's premise of an ideological dialectic, a mode of consciousness that inspires the Western quest for total mastery . . . enables the
development of a quite different perspective on South African history. . . .
Coetzee does not adopt a stance of protest, but of analytical exemplifica-
tion. . . . The whole of Western civilization is implicated in the drive towards
subjugation and mastery. . . . This explains why *protest* is not available to Coetzee
as a strategy: who is protesting to whom? ("Literature and Politics," 126–27)

Thus, the lack of liberal protest, as well as the absence of any sense of
the efficacy of the individual, creates an element of malaise and impasse in Coetzee's fiction.

Magda reflects on the significance of her experiences with Hendrik
and Klein-Anna:

The language that should pass between myself and these people has been subverted by my father and cannot be recovered. What passes between us now is
a parody. I was born into a language of hierarchy, of distance and perspective.
It was my father-tongue. I do not say it is the language my heart wants to speak
. . . but it is all we have. (97)

If the language of hierarchy has been destroyed, what then remains?
Seemingly only chaos, at least for the short term.

Angry that his two-day journey to obtain some of the father's money
at the post office has been a failure, Hendrik verbally abuses Magda
then apparently rapes her. Magda gives multiple versions of the rape
(104–9); in each successive version, Hendrik's and Magda's violence
diminish while Magda's acceptance of the act increases. Her attempt to
attach some meaning to the rape underscores the extreme isolation of
her life: "Am I now a woman? Has this made me into a woman?" (107).
Then soon after, "I long to be folded in someone's arms, to be soothed
and fondled and told I may stop ticking" (108). To that end, she invites
Hendrik and Anna again to move into the house, this time to make
Hendrik's visits to her bedroom less obvious. He does come to her, and
although Magda is affectionate, even solicitous—"Am I doing it right,
Hendrik?" (110)—she does not find the human understanding she seeks.
Hendrik indicated prior to the rape that his motive was revenge: "you
are my wife's half-sister, where your father lay I lie too" (97). She observes that his visits with her become increasingly brief—"sometimes
for only the minute it takes him to release himself inside me" (112)—
and debasing—"He turns me on my face and does it to me from behind like an animal. . . . I am humiliated; sometimes I think it is my
humiliation he wants" (112). Dovey sees the rapes as imaginary attempts by Magda to re-establish the master/slave relationship she lost
with the death of her father: "The repeated fantasies of rape by Hendrik replicate the fantasies of childhood rape by the father, and the

attempt at relationship becomes a fantasy of submission to another master. . . . " (*Novels,* 169).

Whatever the "reality" may be, it is clear that in all of this, Coetzee is drawing the circles of the maelstrom created by the sinking of the massive, hierarchical master/slave society. Magda can no longer ascertain whether Hendrik and Anna are "guests or invaders or prisoners" (112), but she knows that there has been "no transfiguration" (114). Her plea of innocence falls on deaf ears: "I am not simply one of the whites, I am *I*! I am I, not a people. Why do *I* have to pay for other people's sins?" (118). As Watson suggests, even the "colonizer who refuses" shares responsibility as a member of the oppressor group ("Colonialism," 378–79).

After distant neighbors come inquiring about the father, Hendrik and Anna disappear in the night without a word, fearing that they will be blamed for the murder. Now completely solitary, Magda reflects on the significance of these events: "Slaves lose everything in their chains, I recognize, even joy in escaping from them. The host is dying, the parasite scuttles anxiously about the cooling entrails wondering whose tissues it will live off next" (119). She is trapped, without recourse to libertarian solutions, in an era between the demise of the colonial order of her father and the advent of a new order, or chaos, yet to arise.

Twilight in the West

Before proceeding to the conclusion, it would be appropriate to give a synopsis of the issues considered thus far. We have noted the indeterminate nature of the narrative: since Magda's elusive consciousness is the sole delimiter of reality, the novel subverts realism. It also deconstructs the pastoral tradition through the desert isolation of these characters who form a microcosm of the larger isolation of South Africa. We have explored the "beast" in the labyrinth as the master/slave relationships that connect the four principal characters, and we have examined the language of hierarchy versus the language of equality. Finally, we have observed that Magda's murder of her father also constitutes the murder of the old order and that Coetzee does not project the establishment of a new egalitarian order based on libertarian individualism. What remains to be seen is the significance Magda attempts to derive from these experiences in the final pages of the novel.

As the story draws to a close, Magda describes herself as "now truly a mad old bad old woman with a stooped back and a hooked nose with knobby fingers" (123). The images that abound are those of the kind of pestilence found at the opening of Sophocles' *Oedipus Rex* and of the general desolation in Eliot's *Waste Land:* "Winter is coming. . . . The potatoes have gone to seed, the fruit has rotted on the ground. . . .

The pumps spin monotonously day and night" (120); "If one is very patient, if one lives long enough, one can hope to see the day when the last wall falls to dust, the lizard suns itself on the hearth, the thornbush sprouts in the graveyard" (121). In this state of spiritual and physical desolation, Magda undergoes an intense self-examination through the agency of "voices" that speak to her from silver flying machines. The experience—which is a psychological reality for Magda—is necessitated by her isolation: "It is my commerce with the voices that has kept me from becoming a beast. . . . It is not speech that makes man man, but the speech of others" (125–26). Dovey suggests that "like Jacobus Coetzee, she finds that there is no interior to which the self can retreat; that the interior is continuous with the exterior, that the self is Other" (*Novels*, 195).

While it may seem that Magda is just a crazy "mad old bad old woman" ranting to herself, the rhetorical, aphoristic nature of the "messages" from the voices, as well as the linguistic form of Magda's replies to them, are both quite distinct from her earlier utterances. Magda believes that the voices speak to her in Spanish, not "a local Spanish but . . . a Spanish of pure meaning such as might be dreamed of by the philosophers" (126). Here Coetzee the linguist emerges, and rather playfully. When I interviewed him, I asked how he came up with the device of voices of gods speaking to Magda. He replied,

That was just—a great idea—I thought. Spanish? It actually isn't Spanish. I suppose it was really just a joke about universal languages, about what language would the gods speak if they spoke to us. Throughout history there has actually been a lot of—it looks like to me—very comic speculation about what language God speaks.

In addition, the messages of the sky-gods' and Magda's responses are interwoven with paraphrases and quotations from many of the most prominent voices in the literature and philosophy of Western civilization. Dovey mentions Blake, Hegel, and Kierkegaard; my former student Charles Henry identifies correspondences to the writings of Heraclitus, John Calvin, Blaise Pascal, Rousseau, Baron Novalis, Wallace Stevens, Octavio Paz, and Luis Cernuda.[15] Stephen Watson adds to the list Freud, Kafka, Sartre, and Samuel Beckett, and I have noted throughout the prominence of Descartes in Coetzee's thought. Watson asks why Coetzee should so deliberately make his fiction a repository of the most famous thought in the West: "The answer is surely that, divorced from action and its fulfillment in action, thought itself becomes immobilized, petrified, turns into a thing like any other. . . . Even the best thought of the most eminent thinkers becomes worthless." To demonstrate this, Coetzee makes his novel "a veritable museum—in fact, graveyard—of the thought and literary culture of the West" ("Colonialism," 383).

Magda translates into English the messages she receives from the gods, but her words to them are in "Spanish," which Coetzee describes as "a sort of concoction," his own form of Esperanto, which Magda says she "had to invent from first principles, by introspecting" (131). Failing to attract the attention of the gods by shouting, she collects two hundred pumpkin-sized stones with a wheelbarrow and forms her words in letters twelve feet high. This endeavor coming to naught, she records, "And descending to ideographs, I spent all my stones on a sketch of a woman lying on her back, her figure fuller than mine, her legs parted, younger than myself too, this was no time for scrupulosity. How vulgar, I thought to myself . . . yet how necessary!" (134). Like a true postulant, she enhances the sketch with the message, "*FEMM—AMOR POR TU*" (134), and then imagines herself playing Circe to the swinish sky-gods.

While there is certainly an element of "dark humor," as Coetzee phrases it, in this exercise, a reader absorbed in Magda's plight might well read the concluding pages less as a "joke about universal languages" than as a poignant rendering of this woman's aloneness. The effect achieved by rendering Magda's pleas in the linguistic "concoction—an amalgam of Indo-European languages—rather than in English, is similar to that obtained by Eliot in concluding *The Waste Land* with the transliterated Sanskrit, "*Datta. Dayadhvam. Damyata.*" rather than with "Give. Sympathize. Control." One is obliged to pause and reflect.

Deprived of human contact, of a dialectic that leads to a synthesis, and even of any coherent understanding of her own experiences, Magda's messages become desperate pleas for recognition and communion. (In the following, I have attempted to present a coherent English version of Magda's words, without digressing to explicate the numerous linguistic jokes in Coetzee's Esperanto.) Magda presents her supplication to the gods:

ES MI, VENE! ISOLADO! ES MI! VIDI! (131)[16]
It is I, come! I am isolated! It is I! Look!

CINDRLA ES MI; VENE AL TERRA; QUIERO UN AUTR; SON ISOLADO (132)
I am Cinderella; Come to earth; I want an other; Isolated Sound (or Sun, Afrikaans)[17]

POEMAS CREPUSCLRS/CREPUSCULARIAS
Twilight poems

SOMNOS DE LIBERTAD
Dreams of liberty

AMOR SIN TERROR: DII SIN FUROR: NOTTI DI AMITAD
Love without terror: Gods without fury; Signs (or Nights) of friendship/love

[She then responds to the "indictments" of the voices:]

DESERTA MI OFRA—ELECTAS ELEMENTARIAS
A desert you offer me (or, You reject my gifts)—elementary choices

DOMINE O SCLAVA—FEMM O FILLIA
Master or slave—woman/wife or daughter

MA SEMPRE HA DESIDER—LA MEDIA ENTRE (133)
But I have always desired—the medium between

[Receiving no response from the sky-gods, Magda attempts one final solicitation to "*move*" them: she constructs the spread-eagled ideograph enhanced by a twelve-foot high blazon:]

FEMM, FEMM—AMOR POR TU (134)
Woman, woman—love for you

To all of Magda's pleas, the voices are silent, perhaps because, as they state in one of their sibylline utterances, "God loves no one . . . and hates no one, for God is free from passions and feels no pleasure or pain" (134), which is to say that God is simply another manifestation of the "insentient universe" which Magda views as her "purgatory" (67). The responsibility ultimately devolves upon humanity to discover a mode of existence not based on dominance/submission. In one of their most cogent epigrams, the voices address this question in Hegelian terms:

It is the slave's consciousness that constitutes the master's certainty of his own truth. But the slave's consciousness is a dependent consciousness. So the master is not sure of the truth of his autonomy. His truth lies in an inessential consciousness and its inessential acts. (130)

Magda associates this view of the master with her father and longs to escape his entrapped state. While she does not succeed, we should recognize that the Magda who ends the book is not one and the same with the Magda who began it, with her early contradictory narrative, her hatred of self and others, and her deprecating self-descriptions: "a zero, null, a vacuum" (2), "the grim widow-daughter of the dark father" (3), "a miserable black virgin" (5), "the mad hag" (8), "a being with a hole inside me" (9), "a torrent of sound streaming into the universe" (10), "a wire sheathed in crepe" (21), "a cultist of pain" (34), "a poetess of interiority" (35), "a witch-woman" (36), "a black widow in mourning" (40), "a straw woman, a scarecrow" (41), "an O" (41).

At the conclusion of the novel, Magda has not found answers to all of her questions, but her consciousness has altered sufficiently so that she knows the destiny she seeks: "Why will no one speak to me in the true language of the heart? The medium, the median—that is what I wanted to be! Neither master or slave, neither parent or child, but the bridge between, so that in me the contraries should be reconciled!"

(133). She also understands the simplest truth of all: "Where, unless compassion intervenes, does the round of vindictiveness end?" (130). Like some Faulknerian South African Emily, Magda enacts her compassion on the remnants of the father she has killed once in her imagination and once in the flesh, he who is now "a mannikin of dry bones held together by cobwebs" (136). Her perception of her father throughout has been kaleidoscopic: in one view he is "the great No, iron, cold" (51); turn the cylinder and he becomes the well-intentioned Afrikaner, misunderstood; in the final prism of mirrored light, he becomes the repository of fond memories and gentle acts. Although he hears her no more than the sky-gods apparently did, Magda conducts a solitary catechism with him, asking if he recalls their seaside trips, his protective kindness to her when she was a child, how he wept when he had to shoot an aged favorite sheepdog—in effect, the "closing plangencies" (139).

No Messiah appears to fill the void left by the passing of the old order, the old language of hierarchy, which the father represents. The repentant prostitute Mary Magdalene depicted by Luke washed the feet of Jesus with her tears, received forgiveness (7:36–50), and was healed of evil spirits (8:2). Coetzee's Magda anticipates an alien destiny: "God has forgotten us and we have forgotten God. . . . We are the castaways of God as we are the castaways of history. *That* is the origin of our feeling of solitude" (135). Still, Magda does not repudiate her fate. She says she never wished to join the sky-gods but, rather, hoped that they would join her "here in paradise," for she is "corrupted to the bone with the beauty of this forsaken world" (139). She accepts the fact that "for the present, however, it appears that nothing is going to happen, that I may have long to wait before it is time to creep into my mausoleum and pull the door shut behind me . . . " (138).

There should be a term adequate to describe the tone of the ending of *In the Heart of the Country:* inertia, stalemate, deadlock, cul-de-sac, stasis, entropy—conditions common to modern and postmodern literature since Kafka's cockroach first limped on the scene, and certainly characteristic of most Absurdist fiction and drama. But none of these seems appropriate for the ending of Coetzee's exacting depiction of an imagined South Africa at the turn of the century, a foreshadowing of a future which may soon arrive, or of a present which already has.

Coetzee's novel suggests that the apartheid consciousness of the father, and of the old Afrikaner order, is dead, that it is a concept whose time has passed. This story suggests as well that the long suppressed anger of blacks like Hendrik is primed to explode in inarticulate violence, as indeed it has. Nothing alive exists in a state of stasis; the South Africa of the present is in a period of vital, bloody ferment. Those who, like Magda, wish to be neither master nor slave, parent nor child, await a more problematic future. As Coetzee remarked in our interview, "whether it is actually possible for her to escape those dichotomies, I don't know. . . . " The same may be said of all of South Africa's people.

Finally, the term which seems best suited to describe the tone of the ending of *In the Heart of the Country*, as well as the mood of present-day South Africa, is simply "waiting": waiting for the past to return, waiting for the new order, waiting for the apocalypse, waiting for the median, waiting for equality, waiting for Mandela: waiting, perhaps, for Godot, or for the barbarians. In a review article of an anthropological study, *The Whites of South Africa*, Coetzee quotes a passage which provides a fitting conclusion to this chapter: "Wittingly or unwittingly, the whites wait for something, anything, to happen. They are caught in the peculiar, the paralytic, time of waiting. . . . Waiting—the South African experience—must be appreciated in all its banality. Therein lies its pity—and its humanity."[18]

NOTES

1. Stephen Watson, "Colonialism in the Novels of J. M. Coetzee," *Research in African Literatures* 17 (1986): 380.

2. Joan Gillmer, "The Motif of the Damaged Child in the Work of J. M. Coetzee" in *Momentum*, edited by Daymond et al., (Pietermaritzburg: Univ. of Natal Press), 111–12. See also Josephine Dodd, "Naming and Framing: Naturalization and Colonization in J. M. Coetzee's *In the Heart of the Country*," *World Literature Written in English* 27, no. 2 (Autumn 1987): 153–161; Hena Maes-Jelinek, "Ambivalent Clio: J. M. Coetzee's *In the Heart of the Country* and Wilson Harris's *Carnival*," *Journal of Commonwealth Literature* 22, no. 1 (1987): 87–98. Ian Bernard sees Magda as "Coetzee's triumph": "Coetzee, J. M.," in *Postmodern Fiction: A Bio-Bibliographical Guide*, edited by Larry McCaffery (New York: Greenwood Press, 1986), 305–8.

3. Roland Smith, "The Seventies and After," in *Oliver Schreiner and After: Essays on Southern African Literature in Honor of Guy Butler*, edited by Malvern Van Wyk Smith and Don Maclennan (Cape Town: David Philip, 1983), 200.

4. Michael Vaughan, "Literature and Politics: Currents in South African Writing in the Seventies," *Journal of Southern African Studies* 9, no. 1 (1982): 123.

5. See, for example, the previously cited "Waiting for Mandela," "Tales of Afrikaners," "The White Tribe," "Anthropology and the Hottentots," "Blood, Flaw, Taint, Degeneration: The Case of Gertrude Millin," "The White Man's Burden," and "Man's Fate in the Novels of Alex La Guma."

6. Coetzee, in the introduction to his reading from *In the Heart of the Country* in Lexington on 5 March 1984, described it as "a novel set perhaps roughly around the turn of the century in South Africa on a rather isolated farm."

7. J. M. Coetzee, in interview with Stephen Watson, *Speak* 1, no. 3 (1978): 24.

8. Teresa Dovey, *The Novels of J. M. Coetzee: Lacanian Allegories,* Human Sciences Research Council Publication Series, no. 86 (Johannesburg: Ad. Donker, 1988), 150, 156.

9. Paul Rich, "Tradition and Revolt in South African Fiction: The Novels of André Brink, Nadine Gordimer, and J. M. Coetzee," *Journal of Southern African Studies* 9, no. 1 (October 1982): 70.

10. Sheila Roberts, "Character and Meaning in Four Contemporary South African Novels," *World Literature Written in English* 19 (1980): 21.

11. Robert M. Post, "Oppression in the Fiction of J. M. Coetzee," *Critique* 27, no. 2 (1986): 70.

12. André Brink, "Writing Against Big Brother: Notes on Apocalyptic Fiction in South Africa," *World Literature Today* 58, no. 2 (1984): 192.

13. J. M. Coetzee, "Tales of Afrikaners," *New York Times Magazine* 135 (9 March 1986): 75.

14. J. M. Coetzee, "Blood, Flaw, Taint, Degeneration: The Case of Sarah Gertrude Millin," *English Studies in Africa: A Journal of the Humanities* 23 (1980): 52.

15. Charles Henry, "Notes on Magda," unpublished paper.

16. Joe Trahern, my colleague, suggests that this is also an allusion to Caesar's *"veni, vidi, vici,"* in the imperative: "come, see," and by implication, "conquer." I am also indebted for assistance in this translation to my colleagues Professors Michael Handelsman, David Lee, Martin Rice, Chris Craig, and David Tandy.

17. Jan Haluska presents a variant reading of *"SON ISOLADO"*: " 'Son' is the Spanish pronoun 'they,' but in that case the verb should also be plural: *'isolados.'* If this does not simply represent mixed languages, perhaps the mingling of plural and singular indicates that I, you, we, and they, are all intended as possibilities. In that case, 'everybody is isolated' suggests itself as the best reading" (99).

18. Vincent Crapanzano, *The Whites of South Africa* (New York: Random House, 1985); quoted in J. M. Coetzee, "Listening to the Afrikaners—Waiting," *New York Times Book Review,* 14 April 1985, 3.

5

Waiting for the Barbarians:
Sight, Blindness, and
Double-Thought

PROLOGUE

Waiting for the Barbarians is Coetzee's most highly praised and probably his most widely read work. Its mythic yet tangible setting, clarity of characterization, lucid, euphonious prose, and incisive analysis of the colonial mentality make it a major artistic achievement. And yet, as we have seen, *Barbarians* has been criticized for not emphasizing the economic bases of materialism, for not providing solutions to end colonialism, and for a certain quality of malaise, or absence, at its center. Concerning the politically oriented criticism of his fiction, Coetzee had this to say in my interview with him (quoted in part earlier):

I seem to have two sorts of critical publics, one of which is in the United States. . . . The other is in South Africa. And the terms in which these two publics operate . . . are rather different. . . . On the one hand, the body of people in the United States read these books in the general terms in which books are read by intelligent, mainly academic type critics in the U.S. Back in South Africa, there is another type of framework in which they are read, which is very heavily influenced by Marxism, by general Third World thinking. . . . The primary question . . . is, "Where does this book fit into the political struggle?" It is a dominating question there. Those are actually the people I live among. I don't want to disparage them at all . . . they are serious, intelligent people, but they are reading the books in a particular way.

We have already noted representative ideologically based criticism in essays and reviews by Nadine Gordimer, Paul Rich, and Michael Vaughan.[1] Other notable responses to *Barbarians* are to be found in essays by Anthony Burgess, Debra Castillo, Irving Howe, Jane Kramer, Richard G. Martin, Lance Olsen, Roland Smith, George Steiner, and W. J. B. Wood.[2]

The following analysis of *Waiting for the Barbarians* is not basically political in focus, but connections between Coetzee's fictional world and the present state of affairs in South Africa should be apparent. My primary purpose is to demonstrate Coetzee's skillful handling of the leitmotif of blindness and sight: in two of the novel's three principal characters, Colonel Joll and the barbarian girl (sec. 2); in an analysis of the magistrate's Dostoevskian double-thought (sec. 3) and dream visions (sec. 4); and in his subsequent ethical vision (sec. 5).

Coetzee's third novel probably takes its title from the poem "Waiting for the Barbarians" (1904) by the twentieth-century Greek poet Constantin Cavafy.[3] The setting of Cavafy's poem suggests a decadent Roman Empire in decline waiting to capitulate to an anticipated barbarian invasion. However, to the astonishment and confusion of the citizens of the Empire, the barbarians do not appear; the border guards report that "there are no barbarians any longer." The narrator concludes in bewilderment:

> Now what's going to happen to us without barbarians?
>
> Those people were a kind of solution.

In the absence of imminent domination or annihilation by the barbarians, the Empire must face its decadence alone. It has lost the means by which it defined itself as a superior, civilized culture. In Coetzee's novel, the barbarians are the Empire.

Waiting for the Barbarians is set in an indeterminate time and place. The action occurs sometime after the invention of eyeglasses and gunpowder (both of which date from the tenth century A.D.), while the locale cannot be specifically identified. As Coetzee noted in our interview, "The setting is not specified for *Barbarians*, and very specifically is not specified. . . . I just put together a variety of locales and left a lot of things vague with a very definite intention that it shouldn't be pinned down to some specific place." Intentionally, the setting is no-time, no-place, a quality which underscores the allegorical nature of the novel.

At the heart of Coetzee's allegory is a dialectic concerning the relationships between empire and colony, master and slave-rebel, man and woman, blindness and sight, law and barbarism, and expediency and ethics. Stephen Watson has noted: "As is the case with South Africa today, so much of Coetzee's work can be viewed as a failed dialectic, a world in which there is no synthesis, in which the very possibility of a synthesis seems to have been permanently excluded."[4]

COLONEL JOLL AND THE BARBARIAN GIRL:
BLINDNESS AND SIGHT

As an emissary from the capital of the Third Empire determined to crush a rumored barbarian rebellion in a frontier agricultural village, Colonel Joll embodies the consciousness of master/Empire. Unlike the officials in Cavafy's poem, Joll does not passively accept defeat, but aggressively pursues a phantom barbarian force which seems to exist more in his mind than in reality. Undaunted by the absence of a tangible "enemy," Joll and his soldiers torture an old man and his young nephew who say they were coming to the village to seek medical attention for the boy. Either Joll or the soldiers under his command kill the old uncle and torture the boy by twisting a small knife in his skin. Joll's attitude toward this murder and torture reveals the essence of his character: "First I get lies, you see—this is what happens—first lies, then pressure, then more lies, then more pressure, then the break, then more pressure, then the truth" (5).

These actions reveal Joll's barbarian character, which remains consistent throughout the novel and serves as a focal point for the reflections of the narrator, a magistrate who for years has been the lawgiver in the frontier village of about three thousand people and who, prior to Joll's arrival, had looked forward to a quiet retirement. The magistrate (literally, "master") is at once a servant of the same empire that Joll represents and an ethical and humane man who is repelled by Joll's barbarities. In the opening lines of the novel, the magistrate's initial reaction to Joll introduces the theme of sight and blindness: "I have never seen anything like it: two little discs of glass suspended in front of his eyes in loops of wire. Is he blind? I could understand it if he wanted to hide blind eyes. But he is not blind. The discs are dark, they look opaque from the outside, but he can see through them" (1). Joll is ethically blind, as is the empire that he represents; in the capital, he tells the magistrate, everyone wears such glasses. The magistrate's dilemma is that in Joll's dark glasses, he can see a shadowy reflection of himself; thus, he is initially reluctant to censor Joll: "who am I to assert my distance from him? . . . The Empire does not require that its servants love each other, merely that they perform their duty" (5–6). It occurs to him that he could avoid the problem altogether if he simply went on a hunting trip and left the village to Joll's will; he could then return and put his seal on Joll's report after simply skimming it with "an incurious eye." His ethical vision is not sufficiently impaired, however, to allow him this dereliction.

The theme of blindness and sight is further developed after Joll returns to the capital to make his report. As the second section of the novel begins, the magistrate observes a "barbarian" girl begging on the streets. One of Joll's captives, she has been questioned, tortured, and left behind to survive or die. The magistrate sees that her ankles have mended crookedly after having been broken and that she has a strange way of regarding him. As he approaches her, she stares straight ahead, her line of vision at right angles to his approach; as he comes nearer, she gradually turns her head away from him. He makes inquiries and is told that her torturers have blinded her. Under his insistent questioning, the girl reluctantly explains that the soldiers destroyed her frontal vision by holding hot metal prongs close to her lenses. However, she can still see peripherally; thus, she turns her gaze away from the magistrate in order to see him more clearly.

Since all we know of both Joll and the girl comes from the consciousness of the magistrate, we must perceive them through his reports of their actions and words. Joll darkens his vision to conceal himself from the world and, perhaps, to distance himself from his victims. Although the magistrate later struggles to perceive Joll as a sentient being, his first impression of the essence of the colonel's beliefs remains consistent with Joll's actions: "Pain is truth" (5).

The essence of the girl is more obscure. Partially blinded, she makes the best use of the sight that remains to her. Crippled and impoverished in a strange frontier village, she has no means of support but begging and prostitution. She practices both until the magistrate forbids her to beg and offers her (she has no alternative) a position as a domestic in his home. His first perception of her is as a combination domestic and concubine. She is productive as a domestic—"she washes dishes, peels vegetables, helps to bake bread" (32), and later encourages the reluctant magistrate to make love with her.

Most of the magistrate's early thoughts about the girl are attempts to untangle his ambivalent feelings about her and the barbarian culture she represents. Since the two are able to converse only through what she knows of his language (he later laments his shortsightedness in not learning hers), she is an enigma to him and to the reader. We learn only a few facts about her from the magistrate's narrative. He describes her as "a stocky girl with a broad mouth and hair cut in a fringe across her forehead" (73). She has two sisters in her homeland whom she would like to see again. Her father was killed by Joll or his men. Of her past we know little else. More significantly, her manner of "seeing" makes her a foil to the magistrate. Whereas he feels compelled to probe the dark labyrinth of the torturer's mind—he wonders if Joll has a "private ritual of purification, carried out behind closed doors . . . ?" (12)— the girl resists his inquiries about the details of her torture: "Beans make you fart" (29), she replies to his first interrogation. When he finally exacts the details of the blinding from her and then asks, "How do you feel toward the men who did this?" (41), she refuses to respond.

For days they are unable to have sexual intercourse together as the magistrate probes her with questions as her torturers had probed her with their implements: "Are you here in bed with me because it is what you want? . . . Come, tell me why you are here." She replies candidly, "You want to talk all the time. . . . You should not go hunting if you do not enjoy it" (40–41).

Although the girl has virtually no choice but to serve this essentially benevolent master, she is not subservient in spirit. Once he reveals his limited perception of her by making a joke comparing her to a fox cub that he has found: "People will say I keep two wild animals in my room, a fox and a girl" (34). She indicates by her rigid gaze that she does not approve of the comparison, and he apologizes. While the magistrate is torn by conflicting emotions and self-doubt, the girl is stoical. Asked how she survived before he took her in, she readily acknowledges that there were other men. "I did not have a choice. That was how it had to be" (54). When he temporarily stops their sleeping together she accepts this without a word. When he tells her he is going to take her back to her people, she agrees but shows no sign of rejoicing (58). On the excruciating journey across the desert she does not complain. When the accompanying soldiers ostracize her during her menstrual period, "she does not question her exclusion" (70). Most importantly, during his last hours with her, the magistrate sees how clouded his own vision has been in regard to her. Sitting in the tent, he observes her joking with two soldiers by the campfire:

The banter goes on in the pidgin of the frontier, and she is at no loss for words. I am surprised by her fluency, her quickness, her self-possession. I even catch myself in a flush of pride: she is not just the old man's slut, she is a witty, attractive young woman (63).

Thus, in the last moments of their relationship, the magistrate transcends his myopic view of her as servant, concubine, and wild animal.

What can we conclude about the character of this barbarian girl who appears to us dimly through the interstices of the magistrate's doubting eyes? Clearly, in her partial physical blindness, she retains her manner of seeing: she is direct, uncomplaining, independent even in servitude, productive, stoical, convivial, and above all, accepting of things as they are—torturers and lovers, pain and pleasure—without judgment. As Jane Kramer aptly observes, "She yields to everything without yielding herself" ("Garrison," 11).

THE MAGISTRATE: DOUBLE-THOUGHT

The most complex character in Coetzee's novel is the magistrate, who is carrying on a dialectic within himself. Prior to the arrival of Colonel

Joll and the girl, his life had apparently been one of serenity and easy sensuality: administering the law, visiting prostitutes, observing the slow cycle of the seasons, and anticipating a peaceful retirement. Suddenly, a great chasm appears before him, somewhat like the abyss that Conrad's Marlow imagined Kurtz stepping into. As an official of the Third Empire, the magistrate is inevitably linked to Joll. As a humane and just man, he knows Joll has passed into the realm of the forbidden and unclean, into "the horror," as Conrad termed it.

This internal conflict manifests itself in his relationship with the girl. When he takes her into his home he knows immediately that this is at once an act of compassion and coercion: "The distance between myself and her torturers, I realize, is negligible; I shudder" (27). His first act with her—one that he repeats time after time—is in its outward form sacramental: he bathes, massages, and oils her feet and broken ankles, much as Mary, the sister of Lazarus, anointed the feet of Jesus (John 12:1–8) and as Jesus bathed the disciples' feet (John 13:4–5). The magistrate, however, doubts his motives in performing this ritual. The first time that he does it he is aware that while it is a gesture of kindness to the girl, it is also a means of escape for him: "I lose myself in the rhythm of what I am doing. I lose awareness of the girl herself" (28). At other times he resents his "bondage to the ritual of the oiling and rubbing, the drowsiness, the slump into oblivion" (41). He even wishes to "obliterate" the girl, whom he considers "ugly" (47), and sees himself as no better than her torturers: "I behave in some ways like a lover— I undress her, I bathe her, I stroke her, I sleep beside her—but I might equally tie her to a chair and beat her, it would be no less intimate" (43).

Essentially, the magistrate feels guilty because he thinks that in his ministrations to the girl he is attempting to decipher her scars in order to understand their meaning: "Is it then the case that it is the whole woman I want, that my pleasure in her is spoiled until these marks on her are erased and she is restored to herself. . . . Is it she I want or the traces of a history her body bears?" (64). Immediately after this, he questions the validity of all thought: "Or perhaps whatever can be articulated can be falsely put" (64). In this instance, the magistrate becomes very like the "hyperconscious man" that Coetzee discussed in his lecture on Dostoevsky's *Notes from Underground* and *The Idiot*. The hyperconscious person, Coetzee observes, is caught in "an endless cycle of self-consciousness, incessantly questioning his own motives." He notes that Prince Myshkin of *The Idiot* calls this phenomenon "double-thought," literally, "a doubling back of thought." Coetzee contends that "it ought to be possible for people to tell good things about themselves. But this isn't possible for the hyperconscious, because they are always thinking, 'Am I doing this out of vanity?' " However, Coetzee sees a solution to this cycle of double-thought: "self consciousness can be transcended and the endless regression of self-doubt can be overtaken by an overriding will to the truth."[5] It is just such a will to the truth that saves the magistrate from an endless cycle of double-thought and self-recrimination.

In the depths of his sense of self-worthlessness, the magistrate experiences a horrifying vision—"the image of a face masked by two black glassy insect eyes from which there comes no reciprocal gaze but only my doubled image cast back at me" (44). Double-thought has literally become double-vision. In a state of panic, he rebels against his self-destructive impulses:

No! No! No! I cry to myself. It is I who am seducing myself, out of vanity, into these meanings and correspondences. What depravity is it that is creeping upon me? . . . There is nothing to link me with torturers, people who sit waiting like beetles in dark cellars. How can I believe that a bed is anything but a bed, a woman's body anything but a site of joy? I must assert my distance from Colonel Joll! I will not suffer for his crimes! (44)

As we shall see, the magistrate's evolving subconscious vision of the girl will prove to be the key to the labyrinth that will allow him to assert his distance from the torturers.

THE MAGISTRATE: DREAM VISIONS

While the blindness and sight of Colonel Joll and the girl are developed through the physical devices of his dark glasses and her damaged eyes, the magistrate's vision is revealed psychologically. He is certain that he must have seen the girl among the other prisoners before she was disfigured and crippled, but try as he might, the earliest remembrance that he has of her is of the "kneeling beggar girl" (33). The girl, however, tells him that she and the other prisoners all saw him (48). In attempting to recall the girl before she was maimed, the magistrate seems to be trying to envision an Edenic time where torturers have no place. Through the medium of six dreams, he finally achieves his desired vision of the girl before she was tortured.

In all of the dreams but the fourth, snow is used as a chilling, ethereal medium to distinguish the dream world from reality. The magistrate's first dream occurs soon after Joll's arrival but before the magistrate is conscious of having seen the girl. In the dream, children are building a snowcastle in the village square. The magistrate, aware of his "shadowiness" watches all of the children but one melt away from him. She is "older than the others, perhaps not even a child," sitting in the snow with her back to him, "her legs splayed," molding the snow.

When she does not turn around, the magistrate tries "to imagine the face between the petals of her peaked hood but cannot" (9–10). Clearly, this dream foreshadows the frustration he is to experience in reality in trying to remember his first glimpse of her. The second dream occurs after the girl has moved in with him. The village square setting of the first dream is replaced by an "endless plain" covered with snow. Again the other children melt away while the hooded girl builds the snowcastle: "The face I see is blank, featureless; it is the face of an embryo or a tiny whale; it is not a face at all but another part of the human body that bulges under the skin; it is white; it is the snow itself" (37). In the dream, the magistrate repeats the same gesture he made when he first saw the girl begging; he gives her a coin, an act at once suggestive of compassion and guilt.

After agonizing over his motives for caring for the girl and finally purging himself of the double-thought notion that he is simply another Colonel Joll, the magistrate has his third dream about the girl, finally achieving what Coetzee refers to as an "overriding will to truth." In this dream the snow is much deeper than in the others, the air so cold that his "features are frozen" so that he cannot smile or speak. The girl is again building a snow fort. He tries to tell her that she should put people in the empty square, but he is mute, his tongue "frozen like a fish." As she turns toward him, he expects to see again some faceless creature, "But no, she is herself, herself as I have never seen her, a smiling child, the light sparkling on her teeth and glancing from her jet-black eyes. 'So this is what it is to see!' I say to myself" (53). This is the climactic moment of vision in which the magistrate sees the girl as she was in a state of innocence before the torturers came. Soon afterward, he returns her to her people and homeland and he and the girl make love naturally and happily just before they are separated, we presume forever.

His last three dreams of the girl occur after the magistrate has returned to the frontier village and has determined to openly oppose Joll. In the first of these, there is no longer snow, only dust and cold, an appropriate atmosphere for the harsh reality of this dream-nightmare. The Edenic child is gone and the beggar girl is before him, huddled against a wall. He attempts to comfort her and unwraps her bandaged feet, only to discover that they have become nightmarish symbols of the torturer's trade: "The feet lie before me in the dust, disembodied, monstrous, two stranded fish, two huge potatoes" (87). He huddles the detached feet against his body to warm them, then awakens momentarily before re-entering the dream. In this brief segment, Coetzee gracefully captures the essence of the novel:

I enter the barracks gateway and face a yard as endless as the desert. There is no hope of reaching the other side, but I plod on, carrying the girl, the only key I have to the labyrinth, her head nodding against my shoulder, her dead feet drooping on the other side. (87)

If the magistrate knows, as he says in the last line of the novel, that he is traveling on a long "road that may lead nowhere" (156), he knows too that this is the only ethical road to travel and that his compassion for the girl may be his Ariadne's thread to lead him out of the labyrinth and away from Joll's all-consuming Minotaur of hate, back into the light of true vision.

When his fifth dream of the girl occurs, the magistrate has already become the consummate rebel/victim, speaking out against Joll's barbarities, refusing to yield to the impulse of hatred, and suffering the tortures that are the consequence of his rebellion. His nose is broken and his skin welted and bleeding from the blows of a stick as he dreams of the girl. This time she is neither the idealized Edenic girl nor the broken-footed beggar, but simply a lovely girl who lives in a world where no torturers are present. At first he thinks she is again making a "snow-castle or sandcastle," but then he sees that it is a clay oven she has built. She holds out her hands to offer him something. At first he sees it as a "shapeless lump," recalling his early vision of her face, but then he sees that she is offering him a loaf of steaming fresh-baked bread, a gesture as suggestive of a sacrament as his washing and oiling of her feet. Her vesture has religious overtones. She is dressed in a "dark blue robe" and is wearing a "round cap embroidered in gold," while her braided hair has a "gold thread worked into the braid." Overcome by her beauty and her gracious gesture, he sees her as never before: "I have never seen you looking so lovely. . . . Where did a child like you learn to bake so well in the desert?" (109). This is a marked progression from his initial ambivalence about the barbarian girl, whom he finally sees clearly.

Between this and his last dream about the girl, the magistrate subtly, dangerously, mocks Joll's interrogation, is excruciatingly tortured, and then is dressed in women's clothes and derisively hanged from a tree in a mock crucifixion. Finally, he is turned loose as a harmless "fucking old lunatic" (126) to beggar himself in the streets as a mockery to the people to whom he once was the sole administrator of the law. In this clownlike outcast state, with mongrel dogs yelping about him, he tries to console himself with the thought that if he is patient, one day Joll will go away, quiet will return, and Empire will forget this obscure village on the border of his frontier. This passive solution, he realizes, is a delusion: "Thus I seduced myself, taking one of the many wrong turnings I have taken on a road that looks true but has delivered me into the heart of a labyrinth" (136).

He then has his last dream about the girl. The scene is once again the snow-covered square. He begins to walk, but as in the dream-literalism of a Kafka story, the wind-driven snow wafts him aloft. The theme of a vision returns as he sees the solitary girl below his swooping figure: "She will not see me in time!" he thinks, but she does turn and see him: "For an instant I have a vision of her face, the face of a child, glowing, healthy, smiling on me without alarm, before we collide" (136). This is a hopeful dream: "Her head strikes me in the belly; then I am gone, carried by the wind. The bump is as faint as a moth. I am flooded with relief. 'Then I need not have been so anxious after all!' I think. I try to look back, but all is lost from sight in the whiteness of the snow" (136). He awakes, his mouth covered in kisses, not from the girl, but from a stray dog wagging its tail. This jocose-serious moment is but the stuff of dreams, a momentary respite from the harsh reality to follow.

THE MAGISTRATE: ETHICAL VISION

At the core of Coetzee's novel is the magistrate's evolving ethical awareness, which parallels his developing sight in relation to the girl. Although his initial response to Joll's arrival was the temptation to abdicate his position as lawgiver and absent himself, he develops a fascination with the mind of the torturer:

Looking at him I wonder how he felt the very first time; did he, invited as an apprentice to twist the pincers or turn the screw or whatever it is they do, shudder even a little to know at that instant that he was trespassing into the forbidden? . . . Or has the Bureau created new men who can pass without disquiet between the unclean and the clean? (12)

The magistrate himself passes mentally between the unclean and the clean as his fascination with the torturer leads to identification. Like some nineteenth-century nihilist out of Turgenev, he finds the idea of complete leveling destruction a momentarily attractive beginning of reform: "It would be best . . . if these ugly people were obliterated from the face of the earth and we swore to make a new start, to run an empire in which there would be no more injustice, no more pain" (24). Not surprisingly, this flight of fancy is short-lived. In Joll's temporary absence, the magistrate returns to the day to day certainties, administering the law and feeding and healing the prisoners to prepare them for a return to their former lives.

A dramatic change takes place when the magistrate returns to the village after reuniting the girl with her people. He is arrested by Joll's minions for "treasonously consorting with the enemy" (77). Stripped of his magisterial powers and cast into prison, he feels a tremendous sense of elation at being a "free man." His alliance with the empire is over. At the same time, like Camus' Dr. Rieux battling the plague, he maintains his sense of humility: "In my opposition there is nothing heroic— let me not for an instant forget that" (78). His incarceration affords time for reflection and the development of his ethical views: "I should never have allowed the gates of the town to be opened to people who assert that there are higher considerations than those of decency" (81). At the same time, he must not succumb to the same plague that has infected Joll. After seeing a file of "barbarian" prisoners whose hands have been wired to their pierced cheeks, he thinks, "what has become important above all is that I should neither be contaminated by the atrocity that is about to be committed nor poison myself with impotent hatred of its perpetrators. . . . Let it at the very least be said . . . there existed one man who in his heart was not a barbarian" (104).

Soon afterward, his most creative act of rebellion comes in a skillfully dramatized segment. For years the magistrate has pursued a personal quest to excavate some ancient ruins on the outskirts of the village that antedate the extension of Empire into the region. Within the ruins he has discovered about three hundred slips of white poplar wood, each about eight inches by two inches, on which are painted characters in an unknown script. He believes he has identified over four hundred different characters in the script, but after years of study, he still has no idea what they stand for. There is an obvious parallel between the magistrate's failed attempts to "decipher" the scars on the girl and to decode the language on the slips; both remain mysteries to him. Colonel Joll, however, is certain that the magistrate can read the slips and that they are messages from the barbarians; thus, he holds a formal interrogation and demands that the magistrate read the messages. With a self-composure that surprises him, the magistrate imaginatively "translates" the slips, pretending that they describe the atrocities that Joll has committed. As Joll comes to realize that his inquiry is being mocked, the magistrate holds up another slip and suggests that the single character means "war" but that it can also mean "vengeance," or, if turned upside down, "justice," suggesting the perverse interpretation Joll has given to the concepts of truth and justice. For this performance, the magistrate is severely tortured, then deprived of food and water for two days: "They came to my cell to show me the meaning of humanity, and in the space of an hour they showed me a great deal" (115).

In the sixth and last section of the book, the colonel and the magistrate, the man of war and the man of law, have a final, climactic encounter. On unfamiliar terrain, Joll's troops have been routed and slaughtered by the barbarians. Badly in need of mounts and provisions, the ragged survivors return to pillage the frontier outpost before continuing their desperate retreat. In Joll's absence, the magistrate has resumed his position as administrator of law; he is cleanly clothed, his beard trimmed; he has regained a sense of dignity. Joll appears in a state of desperation: his dark glasses are gone; he locks the door of his carriage against the magistrate out of fear. Staring through the window glass of the carriage at the torturer, whom he sees clearly now, the magistrate must struggle against that plague that Camus saw within us all: "An urge runs through me to smash the glass, to reach in and drag the man out through the jagged hole, to feel his flesh catch and tear on the edges, to hurl him to the ground and kick his body to pulp" (146). Ultimately he perceives that it is only through *seeing* the other in the imagination that we are able to overcome such hatred:

His face is naked, washed clean, perhaps by the blue moonlight, perhaps by physical exhaustion. I stare at his pale high temples. Memories of his mother's soft breast, of the tug in his hand of the first kite he ever flew, as well as of those intimate cruelties for which I abhor him, shelter in that beehive. (146)

In this moment of perceptual clarity, the magistrate makes his last attempt to deliver Joll from his murderous blindness:

"The crime that is latent in us we must inflict on ourselves," I say. I nod and nod, driving the message home. "Not on others," I say: I repeat the words, pointing at my chest, pointing at his. He watches my lips, his thin lips move in imitation, or perhaps in derision, I do not know. (146–47)

EPILOGUE

This confrontation is the climax of the novel and of the development of the magistrate's ethical vision. As Camus' Dr. Rieux observed in *The Plague*: "The soul of the murderer is blind; and there can be no true goodness nor true love without the utmost clear-sightedness."[6] The magistrate has attained sufficient vision to overcome his double-thought identification with the torturers through a will to the truth. In his dreams and in his conscious mind he has seen his compassion for the barbarian girl as the key to the labyrinth. He has overcome his hatred by envisioning in Joll the child that became the murderer. These are not slight accomplishments. They argue that "there existed one man who in his heart was not a barbarian" (104). But neither Coetzee nor his magistrate is a facile optimist. Near the end of the novel the magistrate reflects: "To the last we will have learned nothing. In all of us, deep down, there seems to be something granite and unteachable. No one truly believes, despite the hysteria in the streets, that the world of tranquil certainties we were born into is about to be extinguished" (143).

There is no suggestion that the magistrate's entreaties and acts had the slightest effect on Joll or the "barbarians." There is no indication that the public statements and pointed writings of J. M. Coetzee, Alan

Paton, Nadine Gordimer, André Brink, Alex La Guma, Athol Fugard, and others have altered the beliefs of those perpetrating the turmoil in South Africa and elsewhere. In Coetzee's world one makes ethical choices with little expectation of improving the external scheme of things. Rather, such choices make life more bearable moment by moment for the individual in the face of untranquil certainties. In the last scene of *Waiting for the Barbarians*, after Colonel Joll and his defeated troops have retreated to the capital, the frontier village has returned to momentary peace, waiting for the barbarians. The magistrate walks through the square and comes upon several children at play building a snowman, creating the image of humanity. Like a child himself, he is "inexplicably joyful" (155). His final thoughts convey the essence of Coetzee's sense of the human condition:

It is not a bad snowman. This is not the scene I dreamed of. Like much else nowadays I leave it feeling stupid, like a man who lost his way long ago but presses on along a road that may lead nowhere. (156).

NOTES

1. Nadine Gordimer, "The Idea of Gardening," *New York Review of Books*, 2 February 1984, 1–6; Paul Rich, "Apartheid and the Decline of Civilization Idea: An Essay on Nadine Gordimer's *July's People* and J. M. Coetzee's *Waiting for the Barbarians*," *Research in African Literatures*, 15, no. 3 (1984): 365–93; Michael Vaughan, "Literature and Politics: Currents in South African Writing in the Seventies," *Journal of Southern African Studies* 9, no. 1 (1982): 118–38.

2. Anthony Burgess, "The Beast Within," *New York* 15 (26 April 1982): 88–90; Debra A. Castillo, "The Composition of the Self in Coetzee's *Waiting for the Barbarians*," *Critique* 27, no. 2 (Winter 1986): 78–90; Irving Howe, "Waiting for the Barbarians," *New York Times Book Review* 87 (18 April 1982): 1, 36; Jane Kramer, "In the Garrison," *New York Review* 29 (2 December 1982): 8–12; Richard G. Martin, "Narrative, History, Ideology: A Study of *Waiting for the Barbarians* and *Burger's Daughter*," *Ariel* 17, no. 3 (July 1986): 3–21; Lance Olsen, "The Presence of Absence: Coetzee's *Waiting for the Barbarians*," *Ariel* 16, no. 2 (April 1985): 44–56; Roland Smith, "Allan Quartermain to Rosa Burger: Violence in South African Fiction," *World Literature Written in English* 22, no. 2 (1983), 171–82; Roland Smith, "The Seventies and After," in *Olive Schreiner and After: Essays on Southern African Literature in Honor of Guy Butler*, edited by Malvern Van Wyk Smith and Don Maclennan (Cape Town: David Philip, 1983), 196–204, 233; George Steiner, "Master and Man," *New Yorker* 58 (12 July 1982): 102–3; W. J. B. Wood, "*Waiting for the Barbarians*: Two Sides of Imperial Rule and Some Related Considerations," *Momentum: On Recent South African Writing*, edited by M. J. Daymond, et al. (Pietermaritzburg, South Africa: Univ. of Natal Press, 1984), 129–40. This chapter is a revision of my essay, "Sight, Blindness,

and Double-Thought in J. M. Coetzee's *Waiting for the Barbarians*," *World Literature Written in English* 26, no. 1 (Spring 1986): 34–44.

3. Constantin Cavafy (also Kavafis or Kabaphes), *Collected Poems*, translated by Edmund Keeley and Philip Sherrard; edited by George Savidis (Princeton: Princeton Univ. Press, 1975), 31–3.

4. Stephen Watson, "Colonialism in the Novels of J. M. Coetzee," *Research in African Literatures* 17 (1986):382.

5. J. M. Coetzee, taped lecture, Lexington, Kentucky, 5 March 1984.

6. Albert Camus, *The Plague* (New York: Random House, 1948), 121.

6

Life and Times of Michael K: "We Must Cultivate Our Garden"
—Voltaire, *Candide*

SOUTH AFRICA OF THE "NEARER FUTURE"

When *Life and Times of Michael K* appeared in 1983, Coetzee's first three novels had already established his reputation as a fiction writer. Those works received numerous positive reviews in respected publications as well as recognition in literary competitions: South Africa's premier literary prize, the CNA Award (1977, 1980) the Geoffrey Faber Award (1980), and the James Tait Black Memorial Prize (1980), among others. *Michael K* surpassed all of these by receiving England's prestigious Booker-McConnell Prize in 1983.

Michael K is unique among Coetzee's first five novels in several respects: it is the only one to have as its protagonist one of South Africa's disenfranchised majority; the only one to be specifically set in contemporary South Africa; the only one to avoid overt references to racial distinctions; and the only one in which the primary narrator makes no self-conscious reference to the act of narrating. Indeed, *Michael K* seemed to be the novel that would answer the objections of those critics who had faulted Coetzee for not taking a clear political stance in his artistic writing, in the manner of such fellow South Africans as Paton, Gordimer, and Fugard. Robert Post sums up the most frequently expressed reservations: "Coetzee's narratives are inclined to be less straightforward, more ambiguous, and, at least on the surface, not to be about the South Africa of today."[1]

In this regard, Coetzee's own description of *Michael K* is worth noting. He had this to say at a public reading of his works on 5 March 1984, about two months after the novel was published in the United States:

This is a book set in a recognizable South Africa of the—what I think is the—near future, nearer future. It is about Michael K, a young gardener of no particularly distinguished intellect, who has fled the city where everything is falling to pieces under the impact of the war, and has managed to get some kind of garden going again on a deserted farm far from everyone. He lives in a burrow in the ground like an animal and grows all he can grow, namely pumpkins, and living on a diet of pumpkins . . . his strength is rapidly diminishing.

We can summarize the remaining events of the narrative as follows: In part 1 Michael K escapes Cape Town with his mother, intending to take her to the safety of a remote farm where she spent her youth. She dies on the way and K proceeds to the farm with her cremated ashes. He is detained for a time in a labor camp, then arrives at the farm, located near the town of Prince Albert. He buries his mother's ashes on the farm, taking the earth as his symbolic mother, and begins his life as a vegetable gardener.

This existence is disrupted by the arrival of a grandson of the farm's owner, who attempts to make K his servant. K hides in the mountains, barely surviving by eating roots and insects. Near starvation, he walks to Prince Albert and is arrested and taken to Jakkalsdrif, a resettlement camp, where he becomes aware of the plight of other detainees. K escapes and returns to the farm, only to discover that his plants have died without his care. He lives in a burrow in the earth, planting and tending his garden at night. Again near starvation, K is discovered and arrested by soldiers who mistakenly assume he has been supplying food to rebel guerrillas.

Part 2 is narrated by a military medical officer who works at the hospital of the rehabilitation camp where K is imprisoned. The officer becomes obsessed with K and attempts to impose charity upon him, which K passively resists until he escapes from the camp.

In part 3, K is once again in Cape Town. In the war-torn ruins, he encounters some pimps and whores who also treat him as an object of charity. Alone at the end, K envisions a scene in which he helps a derelict old man obtain water. In that way, K would say, "one can live" (184).

In *Life and Times of Michael K*, Coetzee realistically portrays conditions that exist in many of the war-torn areas of South Africa of the recent past and present. There are the smoldering remains of burned-out buildings and overturned lorries and automobiles, smashed store windows, scattered gunfire by riot police and snipers, armed troop carriers, road blocks, crowds huddled under "Relocation" signs, the shrill wail of the curfew siren—in short, the milieu of violence that the world witnessed until Praetoria imposed strict news censorship in 1986.

Michael K's circumstance as the novel opens is that, at thirty-one years of age, he is a "Gardener, grade 1" for the parks service of the City of Cape Town, a job which he abandons when his invalid mother is dismissed from a hospital and asks him to care for her. This he does, joining her in her unventilated, unelectrified, windowless room beneath the stairs leading to the apartment of her former employers (who have fled Cape Town), for whom she worked as a domestic servant. Given the South African setting, the social and economic positions of Michael and his mother, and the fact that they are required to carry a "green card" and a travel permit (which they are never able to obtain), the reader assumes that they are not members of the ruling Afrikaner tribe. On the other hand, the narrative steadfastly avoids any direct mention of race. During my interview with Coetzee, I asked him if he had intentionally excluded racial references from the novel. He replied in part:

Particularly in *Michael K* I am doing that very consciously. The reason, I think, has a lot to do with the over-simplicity of the black/white dichotomy. . . . In South Africa we operate in a situation where everyone is classified in terms of something called the Population Registration Act as belonging to a racial group X, Y, or Z. It is one of the most odious pieces of legislation that exists. It seems to me that any self-respecting piece of writing that goes along with this thinking behind the P. R. A.—which is that everyone is born into a certain race—that's not actually the way that writing ought to work. . . . In any event, I don't think that one should, in a book like my book, portray from the inner-consciousness of someone, someone who thinks of himself as being fated to be whatever he is.

Despite Coetzee's fastidious silence about race, it becomes apparent to the reader—if only from the masterly way in which authority figures speak to Michael—that he is not "white." Nadine Gordimer says that the fact that Michael's mother is a house servant in Cape Town indicates that in South Africa he would be classified as a "so-called coloured."[2] However, as Coetzee stated in our interview, "Other people in the book can think of him what they want. The important thing is that he doesn't." As a result, the racial issue is muted in a way that sets this novel apart from comparable works by Gordimer, Brink, Fugard, and others. One tends to think of Michael K more in terms of his individuality than as a representative of any group.

K the Outsider: The Kafka Connection

Michael K's distinct individuality is closely connected to his role as outsider, the individual who prefers solitude to the company of others, from whom he often feels estranged. K is set apart physically by his disfiguring harelip and gaping left nostril, to which our attention is drawn repeatedly throughout the narrative. This deformity so repelled his mother that she placed him in a state school, Huis Norenius in Faure, where, until the age of fifteen, he spent his time in the company of other rejected and afflicted children. Michael's isolation is underscored by his conception of the school's regimentation and its abusive teachers: "My father was the list of rules on the door of the dormitory" (104–5).

A number of factors have prompted critics to associate Michael K with Kafka's heroes: his estrangement and isolation, his embattlement with authority/father figures, and the patronymic K. Teresa Dovey places *Michael K* in the genre of "the novel of the inarticulate victim"[3] and connects Michael specifically with Kafka's Joseph K. of *The Trial* and K. of *The Castle*, noting that all three are "the dispossessed ones . . . victims of the process" (265). She points out that "the Castle" mentioned in *Michael K* is probably at once an allusion to Kafka's novel and a reference to "the actual military headquarters situated in the castle built at the time of the early Dutch settlement at the Cape" (302). She further notes that the burrow which Michael inhabits on the farm replicates the dugout in Kafka's story "The Burrow," which Coetzee explicated in an essay published two years before *Michael K* appeared, "Time, Tense and Aspect in Kafka's 'The Burrow.'" Robert M. Post also notes most of these Kafkaesque elements in his article on the theme of oppression in Coetzee's first four novels ("Oppression," 66–77), while Nadine Gordimer dismisses the Kafka connection altogether, stating that the initial *K* "probably stands for Kotze or Koekemoer and has no reference, nor need it have, to Kafka" ("Idea," 3). Coetzee himself rejected the Kafka connection in 1983 when he told an interviewer, "I don't believe that Kafka has an exclusive right to the letter K. Nor is Prague the center of the universe."[4]

Nevertheless, the Kafka relics (or tributes) to be found in Coetzee's *Michael K* seem too obvious to be coincidental, but they are not particularly substantive. For one thing, the theme of oppression is too pervasive in literature to be specific to any author. The most viable parallel is between Michael K and the protagonist of Kafka's "A Hunger Artist," a connection which Dovey makes (*Novels*, 30). Both characters are capable of surviving incredibly long periods of fasting, but with very different motivations. When Michael is hiding in the mountains, he at first eats whatever comes to hand—roots, bulbs, ant-grubs, flowers— after which he fasts until he reaches a state where he "emptied his mind, wanting nothing, looking forward to nothing" (68–69). When he realizes "that he might die" of starvation he comes down from the mountain seeking food. Near the end of the novel when he is incarcerated in a military hospital, he fasts as a protest against the "charity" that the medical staff tries to impose on him and because he does not like the food. When he is brought a squash, which he likes, he readily eats it. The doctor remarks—in what seems to be an obvious allusion to Kafka—"You were not a hero and did not pretend to be, not even a hero of fasting" (163).

In contrast, Kafka's hunger artist makes a career of fasting, enter- taining the disbelieving gawkers from within the bars of his guarded cage, until his impresario forces him to come out each time at the end of forty days, not for reasons of health, but of profit, since public in- terest in the feat wanes after that length of time. When public fasting becomes passé, the hunger artist winds up in a cage in a zoo where he is promptly forgotten, concealed behind bales of hay. There he proba- bly breaks all fasting records, but no one knows because no one keeps track of his fasting time, not even the hunger artist. Near death, he asks the few onlookers to "forgive" him. He fasted, he tells them, be- cause he wanted them to admire him (implicitly, for his restraint and endurance), but they should *not* admire him, he says, because his real reason for fasting was that he could not help himself—"because I couldn't find the food I liked. If I had found it, believe me, I should have made no fuss and stuffed myself like you or anyone else."[5] This is classic Kafka: for the hero to attain his desire (admiration, appetizing food, love of life) is an impossibility; his art, if carried to perfection, inevita- bly leads to death, in this instance, to a passive death.

Coetzee's gardener, in contrast, evidences a resolute will to live and to make the earth bountiful. When he fasts, it is because he chooses to eat what he has grown: "When food comes out of the earth, he told himself, I will recover my appetite, for it will have savor" (101). Fasting also appears to contribute to a sense of joyful transport: "there was nothing but bone and muscle on his body. . . . Yet as he moved about his field he felt a deep joy in his physical being. . . . It seemed possible to fly; it seemed possible to be both body and spirit" (101–2). When he does eat the food he has grown—in the following instance, the first of his pumpkins—his pleasure borders on delirium: Michael "felt his heart suddenly flow over with thankfulness. . . . Beneath the crisply charred skin the flesh was soft and juicy. He chewed with tears of joy in his eyes. The best, he thought, the very best pumpkin I have tasted" (113). Despite the surface similarities, Coetzee's Michael K, in his essence, is at the opposite end of the spectrum from the Kafka hero, who is doomed from the outset to a joyless and unfulfilled life, the hunger artist, wait- ing for death in the last ditch of velleity.

The Dawn of Consciousness: Invention, Ethics, Self-Reflection

Michael K is further set apart from the calculating, perspicacious heroes of *The Trial* and *The Castle* by his slowness of mind. After convincingly depicting the obsessive and sometimes psychotic thought-processes of Eugene Dawn and Jacobus Coetzee, the labyrinthine broodings of Magda, and the philosophical reflections of the magistrate, Coetzee has again demonstrated his versatility by revealing in Michael K the awakening consciousness of a primitive mind. In the writers' workshop which Coetzee conducted on 6 March 1984, in Lexington, one of the participants observed that the primary narrator of *Michael K* employs "a very odd kind of omniscience, as if it were rooted in the individual's [Michael's] character." Coetzee responded:

It's a mixture. It's a fluctuation in and out. There is a—if I can use an oxymoron—a limited omniscient point of view operating in part 1 of that book. That is to say, there is someone who is telling the story about Michael K, who looks like an omniscient narrator, but he doesn't actually tell you very much. And . . . there is no guarantee that he knows very much.

Thus, the main narrator exercises a certain reserve, usually limiting narrative observations to those which Michael is capable of perceiving. The prose style, too, is basic and straightforward, eschewing the intricate syntax and metaphors that characterize Coetzee's earlier works. This narrative style is appropriate, since Michael, along with the barbarian girl, is one of Coetzee's two least articulate characters, after Friday in *Foe*, who cannot speak at all.

The narrative and stylistic elements are illustrated in descriptions of some major changes of awareness that Michael undergoes. For example, he finds the physical intimacy of his mother's small, dingy room unpleasant: "But he did not shirk any aspect of what he saw as his duty. The problem that had exercised him years ago behind the bicycle shed at Huis Norenius, namely why he had been brought into the world, had received its answer: he had been brought into the world, to look after his mother" (7). When his mother suggests that they should travel approximately 270 miles overland in a war-torn country without proper permits and, as it turns out, with no mode of transportation but a wheelbarrow, Michael "accepted without question the wisdom of her plan for them" (8–9). Coetzee also conveys Michael's cognition through visual imagery: "He saw, not the banknotes spread on the quilt, but in his mind's eye a whitewashed cottage in the broad veld with smoke curling from its chimney, and standing in the front door his mother, smiling and well" (9). Such innocent romanticism on Michael's part is reminiscent of John Steinbeck's retarded character Lennie, who, in *Of Mice and Men*, is sustained by his dreams of a "piece of lan' " and a rabbit farm. Coetzee, like Steinbeck, runs the risk that his portrait of primal innocence may be perceived as comic stupidity.

Coetzee's Michael K, however, is characterized to a much greater extent by his thought-processes than is Steinbeck's Lennie, although both are portrayed in a naturalistic mode emphasizing their affinity for and similarity to animals. While slow of wit, Michael is a man of great patience who uses his imagination to invent solutions to the problems that confront him. An excellent example occurs early in the novel when he has to find a mode of transportation to carry his mother from Cape Town to Prince Albert. Michael remembers a wheelbarrow in a storage shed and breaks in and takes it. He persuades his mother to ride in it and is disconcerted to discover how unwieldy it is bearing her weight. He thinks the wheels from his bicycle would improve the balance, "but he could not think where to find an axle" (11). Several days later, he comes upon a scrapyard and buys a steel rod one meter long. He returns to his project and finds that while the rod fits snugly into the wheel bearings, "he had no way to prevent the wheels from spinning off. For hours he struggled without success to make clips out of wire. Then he gave up. Something will come to me, he told himself" (16). As the violence increases in Cape Town during the next few days, he returns to the problem of keeping the wheels on and finds a solution: "He worked all afternoon; by evening, using a hacksaw blade, he had painstakingly incised a thread down either end of the rod, along which he could wind clumps of one-inch washers" (18). He completes the project by adding a plastic canopy and shifting the center of gravity: "Since the first trip he had moved the axle two inches forward; now, once he got it going, the cart was as light as a feather" (24). Even this compressed version of the episode illustrates Michael's steadfast determination. While he is slow-witted, he is not without invention.

While there are many other examples of Michael's ingenuity—particularly in growing and concealing his vegetables, and himself—Coetzee also develops aspects of Michael's self-awareness, particularly with regard to ethics, cognition, and being. Ethical considerations do not often concern Michael, but a few instances stand out. On the road alone after his mother's death, he adopts an animal-like existence, scavenging what food he can, including half-spoiled fruit, "taking bites of good flesh here and there, chewing as quickly as a rabbit, his eyes vacant" (39). Coetzee tempers Michael's creature-nature by having him reflect that taking the fruit from a farmer's land may be stealing. In contrast to such double-thinking characters as Magda and the magistrate, Michael cuts through the ethical question quickly: "It is God's earth, he thought, I am not a thief" (39). On the other hand, when a man who befriends

Michael suggests "people must help each other," Michael reflects upon, but does not resolve the question: "Do I believe in helping people? he wondered. He might help some people, he might not help them, he did not know beforehand, anything was possible. He did not seem to have a belief, or did not seem to have a belief regarding help" (48). Thus, he perceives a category of ethical consideration but avoids accepting an absolute principle when the context of choice is not known.

On the other hand, when he must choose a path of action within a specific circumstance, he can act deliberately. The burial of his mother's ashes that he has carried to the farm is charged with significance for Michael. He meditates, "hoping that a voice would speak reassuring him that what he was doing was right—his mother's voice, if she still had a voice . . . or even his own voice as it sometimes spoke telling him what to do. But no voice came. So he extracted the packet from the hole, taking the responsibility on himself, and . . . he distributed the fine grey flakes over the earth" (59). Clearly, Coetzee's slow-witted gardener thinks with more clarity and deliberateness than many of his more cerebral thought-tormented characters.

Michael also reflects on the nature of cognition. After exhausting himself killing a goat, only to discover that the flesh repells him, he attempts to draw significance from the event: "The lesson, if there was a lesson, if there were lessons embedded in events, seemed to be not to kill such large animals" (57). Similarly, toward the end of the novel, he considers the meaning of his experiences: "(Is that the moral of it all, he thought, the moral of the whole story: that there is time enough for everything? Is that how morals come, unbidden, in the course of events, when you least expect them?)" (183). Coetzee's carefully controlled narration allows us to follow the evolution of Michael's consciousness without an obtrusive intermediary.

Even more than questions regarding ethics and cognition, the nature of being preoccupies Michael. He considers the relation of life to death and perceives a duality: He hopes that his mother, "who was in some sense in the box and in some sense not, being released, a spirit into the air, was more at peace now that she was nearer her natal earth" (57). At the same time, he projects the disposition of his physical being after his death in a memorable image: "If I were to die here, sitting in the mouth of my cave looking out over the plain with my knees under my chin, I would be dried out by the wind in a day, I would be preserved whole, like someone in the desert drowned in sand" (67–68). But it is life and nurturing that absorbs his attention most. Upon planting his mother's ashes in the earth, he has an awakening concerning the essence of his being: "It is because I am a gardener, he thought, because that is my nature. . . . There were times, particularly in the mornings, when a fit of exultation would pass through him at the thought that he, alone and unknown, was making that deserted farm bloom" (59). He is no longer the kind of gardener he had been with the parks department in Cape Town, tending well-kept lawns, but a gardener, a parent of plants, one so closely allied with the earth that his nature is transformed: "I am becoming a different kind of man, he thought, if there are two kinds of man. If I were cut, he thought, holding his wrists out, looking at his wrists, the blood would no longer gush from me but seep, and after a little seeping dry and heal" (67).

Such self-conscious reflections come only occasionally to Michael, and he bears them at a certain cost: "Always, when he tried to explain himself to himself, there remained a gap, a hole, a darkness before which his understanding balked, into which it was useless to pour more words" (110). For this man who finds articulation with others intimidating and with himself baffling, the best communication is that of silence, of being without words, of work without effort. He learns to love idleness, not as stolen moments of private pleasure, but "as a yielding up of himself to time, to a time flowing slowly like oil from horizon to horizon over the face of the world. . . . He was neither pleased nor displeased when there was work to do; it was all the same" (115).

The simple-mindedness of Coetzee's humble gardener may be illusory, for Michael's beliefs are very much in harmony with the wisdom of the sixth-century B.C. sage, Lao Tsu, who taught that "Teaching without words and work without doing / Are understood by very few." And again, "Keep your mouth closed. . . . Be at one with the dust of the earth / This is primal union."[6] Put another way, to be involved with *being* is the path to understanding.

Being Versus Becoming: Sticks and Stones

Stephen Watson has pointed out that in Coetzee's first four novels, all of the protagonists except Michael K "beat against the shackles of their historical position in vain."[7] Eugene Dawn, Jacobus, Magda, and the magistrate are all fated to think and "think to no end." Trapped in insoluble dilemmas, they "begin succumbing to the attractions of a world of being as opposed to a world of becoming" (384). "Being" in this context means the capability of existing in oneself, as a stone exists, outside the forces of history and time; "becoming" is acting within the historical moment; as Watson says, to become a participant in "a world of event . . . in which there is direction and purpose" (386).

In each of his novels, Coetzee has placed his central characters in a relationship with inanimate stones or sticks to illuminate the characters' potential for being or becoming. The stone imagery associated with Eugene Dawn suggests sterility and impotence. He remembers as a boy growing a crystal garden which he observed through the glass walls of

a jar, "stalagmites obeying their dead crystal life-force." In contrast to
Michael K, he is incapable of growing the "other kind" of seeds; the
beans he plants rot (30). As we have already seen, Jacobus in his dy-
namic psychic journey is intrigued by the desert stones and longs to
explore their interiors. However, beneath his explorer's hammer, a
stone's interior transforms itself into exterior, and the mysteries of the
stone's being escape him, become "fictions, these lures of interiors for
rape which the universe uses to draw out its explorers" (78). The stones,
he decides, "so introverted, so occupied in quietly being, were after all
my favorites" (96), but Jacobus in his lust for vengeance, has no time
to enter into the world of being, for he must resume his furious journey of masterhood.

Magda, who lives "in the dead centre of the stone desert" (129), is
torn between her desire for a life of "event," or becoming, and its opposite: "I am lost in the being of my being. This is what I was meant
to be: a poetess of interiority, an explorer of the inwardness of stones"
(35). She goes so far as to contemplate entering a stonelike existence:
"Though I may ache to abdicate the throne of consciousness and enter
the mode of being practiced by goats or stones, it is with an ache I do
not find intolerable" (26). Ultimately, her desire for human communication and understanding leads her to reject this possibility: "I hold
the goats and stones . . . suspended in this cool, alienating medium of
mine, exchanging them item by item for my word-counters. . . . Words
alienate" (26). As we have seen, her efforts at the end of her story are
not to enter into a realm of being, like the stones, but to turn the stones
into signifiers, so that she may communicate with the sky-gods and escape her miserable isolation. To this end she collects a pile of two
hundred stones, "smooth, round, the size of small pumpkins" (132),
anticipating Michael K.

The magistrate in the end realizes that he "wanted to live outside
history" (154). He asks, "What has made it impossible for us to live in
time like fish in water, like birds in air, like children? It is the fault of
Empire! Empire has created the time of history" (133). Unable to attain
a life of being or to escape his role in the historical world of event, he
attempts to decipher history by reading the enigmatic wooden slips he
has discovered buried in the sand dunes among the remnants of the
forgotten civilization that created the slips. Despite his efforts, the poplar slips do not yield their essence to the magistrate any more than did
the interiors of stones to Jacobus. Failing to decipher their message,
the magistrate utilizes the wooden slips as signifiers to communicate
with Colonel Joll (110–12), as Magda utilized the stones to communicate with the sky-gods.

Of the protagonists in Coetzee's first four novels, only Michael K can
be said to have escaped historical event to enter a realm of being out-

side of linear time. Rather than attempt to penetrate the mysteries of stones, as Jacobus does, or permute them, as Magda does, Michael from the beginning identifies with stones: "Perhaps I am the stony ground" (48) he thinks, or "a speck upon the surface of an earth too deeply asleep to notice the scratch of ant-feet" (97); "let the earth swallow me up and protect me" (107) he asks. Unlike the magistrate, who attempts to impose meaning even on "three specks on the wall" of his cell—"*Do they stand for anything?*" (84)—Michael is content to let things *be* without meaning. Staring at the rust-tracings on the corrugated roof of his barrow, "he would see nothing but the iron, the lines would not transform themselves into pattern or fantasy; he was himself, lying in his own house, the rust was merely rust, all that was moving was time, bearing him onward in its flow" (115). Unlike Magda, who believes that "it is the first condition of life forever to desire" and who speculates that "only stones desire nothing" (114), Michael is described as having "emptied his mind, wanting nothing, looking forward to nothing" (69), and at another point, as feeling "a deep joy in his physical being" (102). It is his physical being which sets the outer limits of his ability to be detached from all desire: "You are forgetting to breathe, he would say to himself, and yet lie without breathing" (118). After a long fast, it occurs to him that "he might die, he or his body, it was the same thing" (69). He achieves what the magistrate desires but could not attain—to live in the cyclical time of nature: "He lived by the rising and setting of the sun, in a pocket outside time" (60). Again we are told, "he was living beyond the reach of calendar and clock in a blessedly neglected corner, half awake, half asleep. Like a parasite dozing in the gut, he thought, like a lizard under a stone" (116).

It is the medical officer in part 2 who provides an external view confirming Michael's unique existence: "He is like a stone, a pebble that, having lain around quietly minding its own business since the dawn of time, is now picked up and tossed randomly from hand to hand. A hard little stone . . . enveloped in itself and its interior life. He passes through these institutions . . . like a stone. Through the intestines of war" (135). The medical officer, harried by the exigencies of historical event, recognizes that Michael has "managed to live in the old way, drifting through time, observing the seasons, no more trying to change the course of history than a grain of sand does" (152).

Michael K's success in escaping the forces of history has prompted some troubled responses among South African critics and authors. Stephen Watson asks, "What sort of model does he provide for we, readers, who have to live *in* history and could not survive elsewhere? . . . Is Michael K's achievement (for the time being) really enough?" ("Colonialism," 389–90). Similarly, Nadine Gordimer praises Coetzee's moving depiction of "what white has done to black" in South Africa, but questions his putting such a passive individual at the center of this novel: "For is there an idea of survival that can be realized entirely outside a political doctrine?" ("Idea," 6). Nevertheless, she concludes that Michael K's idea of gardening is the real point: "Beyond all creeds and moralities, this work of art asserts, there is only one: to keep the earth alive, and only one salvation, the survival that comes from her" (6). In an interview given the same year that *Michael K* was published (1983), Coetzee asserts the primacy of artistic conception over political reality. Acknowledging that he knew he would be at risk in making Michael K the central figure of the novel, he contends, "But then it didn't turn out to be a book about *becoming* . . . but a book about *being*, which merely entailed that K go on being himself, despite everything" (Morphet interview, 455).

My own view is, perhaps it is just possible, that there is a condition or place in which one is in both a state of being and becoming, either concurrently or alternately: a state in which one is aware of who one is, the stone in the desert, and at the same time, a stone moving among stones in a world of event and change.

Coetzee's Adaptation of the *Plaasroman* and Agrarian-Protest Novel

Gordimer is quite right to conclude that one of the central concerns—perhaps the primary concern—of *Life and Times of Michael K* is humanity's relation to the earth, to gardening, to the farm. It is surprising that, in the criticism published about the novel thus far, so little attention has been given to this subject. We have already seen how *In the Heart of the Country* can be read as a subversion of the idyllic farm novel. In addition, Coetzee has evidenced considerable interest in and erudition concerning the farm in history and in fiction. He has published an anthropological study of the European agriculturists' view of the "idleness" of the Hottentots, studies of farm novelists Pauline Smith and C. M. van den Heever, and most recently, an essay entitled "Farm Novel and *Plaasroman*."[8]

In the latter essay, Coetzee focuses on the farm novels of Olive Schreiner and Pauline Smith but evidences a broad understanding of the fictional genre as well as a knowledge of farming's mythology, history, ecology, sociology, and economics: precapitalist societies, barter economies, patriarchal capitalism, the effects of primogeniture, labor practices in European peasant and colonial societies, as well as Jeffersonian and Marxian views of agriculture. While Coetzee does not often stress economic and material factors in his fiction, he certainly has an understanding of these issues. Our concern here, however, is specifically with the *plaasroman*, or farm novel. Coetzee stresses the pervasiveness of the genre: "For two decades of this century, 1920–1940, the Afrikaans novel concerned itself almost exclusively with the farm and *platteland* (rural) society" (63); also, he notes, among the major English-language novelists in South Africa, Olive Schreiner and Pauline Smith have concentrated on farm life in their fiction. He points out that "nostalgia for country life . . . is a feature of a great deal of writing in England in the years up to 1939" (75), and that in Germany between 1929–38, almost two hundred "return to the land" novels were published (76). In the same essay he observes that one of the characteristics of the Afrikaans *plaasroman* and the novels of Schreiner and Smith is a "silence about the place of black labour," which "represents a failure of imagination before the problem of how to integrate the dispossessed black man into the idyll . . . of African pastoralism" (71–72). These silences, he observes, "speak more loudly to us than they did fifty years ago. Our ears today are finely attuned to modes of silence" (81). Coetzee credits Nadine Gordimer's *Conservationist* (1977) with having laid the ghost of the "pastoral solution to the question of how the white man shall live in South Africa . . . that he should retreat into rural independence" (81). Gordimer's novel, which opens with a graphic description of the body of an unidentified black man, presents "the dark side of farm life, its buried half, the black corpse in the garden" (81). We can add that *Life and Times of Michael K* "lays the ghost" of silence regarding the black man's relation to the earth, not through the agency of a corpse, but by its moving portrait of Michael's steadfast and gentle nurturing of his plants, which he regards as his "children."

While Coetzee's fourth novel bears an important relation to English South African, Afrikaans, German, and English farm novels, it also has a strong resemblance to certain features of the American agrarian-protest novel in the tradition of Hamlin Garland, Frank Norris, and Louis Bromfield, the latter of whom Coetzee discusses briefly in his "Farm Novel" essay (76). As I shall demonstrate, *Life and Times of Michael K* has some significant correspondences to the most widely known novel in this genre, John Steinbeck's *Grapes of Wrath* (1939).[9] In response to my question about his knowledge of Steinbeck's novel, Coetzee replied in his letter of 14 August 1987, "I have read *The Grapes of Wrath*, but I don't know one way or the other whether I read it 'intently' (does one always know?)." Although I will point out a number of striking similarities, and some differences, between the two novels, I do not suggest that Coetzee's work is in any sense derived from Steinbeck's; rather, both authors found some form of the same genre suitable to their purposes and times.

In his farm novel essay, Coetzee points out that "the Great Depression provoked alarm about rural depopulation and agitation for a return to the land in many countries" and that novels of the Depression stressed the importance of "instinctualism, tilling the soil as a quasi-religious act in a . . . [living space] free from capitalistic relations, subject only to natural laws" (76).

Both *The Grapes of Wrath* and *Life and Times of Michael K* are set against a background of social turmoil in which the dispossessed tillers of the soil are oppressed by the powers of industrial capitalistic societies. In Steinbeck's novel the banks seize the land of the farmers in the wake of drought and worldwide economic collapse. The hostilities between the two groups are manifested in armed clashes between migrants and police, the starvation of children and adults, murder, and the underlying theme of "wrath" in the narrative. *Michael K*, as we have seen, is set against a background of civil war in which rebels have taken up arms against government military forces and, as in Steinbeck's novel, "the army of the homeless and destitute" (13) have inundated the cities seeking work and food: "entire families had been turned off the farms they had lived on for generations" (79).

In each novel the central characters determine to leave the barren land of their homes and journey to what they believe is an Edenic paradise. The Oklahoma migrants are told that California is a place of bounty. Michael K's mother longs to return to the farm of her youth, which she remembers as a place of "warmth and plenty" where she found nests of chicken eggs "under blue skies" (8). As noted earlier, Michael readily accepts this dream. In Steinbeck's novel, the Joad grandparents die on the road before reaching their promised land; the same fate takes Michael K's mother.

The Bonding of the Dispossessed

The hardships of the journey to "paradise" and the destitution of the travelers in each case lead to a bonding between the dispossessed, a movement "from 'I' to 'we' " (165), as Steinbeck's narrator says. Although Michael K is an outsider by nature and a loner by preference, his experiences in sharing among the destitute are much the same as the Joads. Before he and his mother set out on the road he assures her, and himself, "People were decent, people would stop and give them lifts" (18), which is borne out a few pages later when a man in a lorry gives them a ride (24). At the hospital where he takes his mother, he mentions that he is hungry, and a man whom Michael does not know buys him a hot meat pie. The narrator underscores the bonding: "He sat beside his friend on the bench and ate. The pie was so delicious that tears came to his eyes" (30). When Michael is on the road alone, a man invites him to a dinner of soup and pan-bread with his family. Michael says that he has been warned that land owners will shoot trespassers: "His friend shook his head. 'I've never heard of that,' he said. 'People must help each other, that's what I believe' " (48). Later, in the Jakkalsdrif resettlement camp, a woman risks punishment to pass him some soup (77), paralleling Ma Joad's sharing a portion of her family's stew with hungry children (284). Michael evidences his own sense of sharing by giving portions of his food and pay to a man named Robert, whose family is with him in the camp (84). Finally, K's last thoughts in the novel are of nurturing an old man with scarce water, a counterpart to Rose of Sharon's eucharistic giving of the milk of her breasts to the starving old man at the conclusion of Steinbeck's novel.

In both novels the government provides "camps" for the homeless which afford them immediate relief at the cost of deferring their ultimate goal, obtaining land to farm. To the Joads, the government camp initially offers blessed relief from life on the road: a protected environment, running water (showers, flush toilets), community, social life—all for one dollar per week or the equivalent in work. On the other hand, there is no work available in the nearby community. In South Africa, Jakkalsdrif is also a "camp for people without jobs" (78), and offers running water, shelter, and food, but only to those who work as cheap labor for the railroad and for farmers with political influence. The inmates are in effect subject to enforced labor, but there are other camps offering harsher options: "penal servitude, hard labour, brickfields, guards with whips" (78), so that one inmate refers to Jakkalsdrif as "our Welfare" (79). As in Steinbeck's novel, the townspeople of neighboring Prince Albert regard the camp as a hotbed of subversive activity, and, after a fire breaks out in the town, the police savagely attack the camp, beating those who live there and turning the site into a "trashheap."

Soon after this, Michael begins to reflect on the ideas of the man named Robert, who became politicized after he and his family of eight were turned off of a farm where he had worked for twelve years (79). Robert explains to Michael that the police had arrested him and his family on the road for having "no fixed abode" (80) the day after he had been fired, and brought them to Jakkalsdrif. Robert believes that such camps exist for two reasons: because the people would otherwise join the guerrilla rebels in the mountains (80) and "because we look too terrible when we get sick and die. If we just grew thin and turned into paper and then into ash and floated away, they wouldn't give a stuff for us. . . . They want to go to sleep feeling good" (88). When Michael, inarticulate and apolitical, does not know how to respond, Robert castigates him: "You're a baby. . . . You've been asleep all your life. It's time to wake up. . . . Because they think you are harmless, your eyes aren't opened, you don't see the truth around you" (88–89).

After a violent sacking of the camp and attack on the inmates by the police, Robert predicts that the officials will starve them to death, "lock us up and wait for us to die" (94).

At this point, Michael's beliefs begin to undergo a transformation, as did Tom Joad's through Jim Casy's example:

K brooded on Robert's words. He no longer found it so strange to think of the camp as a place where people were deposited to be forgotten. . . . If these people really wanted to be rid of us, he thought (curiously he watched the thought begin to unfold itself in his head, like a plant growing), if they really wanted to forget us forever, they would have to give us picks and spades and command us to dig; then, when we had exhausted ourselves digging . . . they would have to break down the huts and the fence and tents as well as every last thing we had owned upon us, and cover the earth, and flatten the earth. *Then*, perhaps, they might begin to forget about us. But who could dig a hole as big as that? (94)

After arriving at this metaphor of perverse planting, Michael realizes, as did Tom Joad, that his teacher's thoughts have sprung to life inside him. Tom is surprised to discover that he has taken on Casy's beliefs: "God, I'm talking like Casy. Comes of thinkin' about him so much" (463). Similarly, Michael reflects, "It seemed more like Robert than like him, as he knew himself, to think like that. Would he have to say that the thought was Robert's and had merely found a home in him, or could he say that though the seed had come from Robert, the thought, having grown up inside him, was now his own? He did not know" (95). Coetzee does not develop Michael's political consciousness further, aside from his resistance to manipulation by the medical officer near the end of the story, for Michael, the tender of the earth, prefers the company of plants, or solitude, to that of people and causes.

"The Bounty of the Earth"

The Grapes of Wrath and *Michael K* both have naturalistic elements in that they view human beings in the context of the animal kingdom and in relation to the earth. Steinbeck early in his novel connects the western trek of the migrants with the determined movements of a turtle, broadcasting and covering seeds along its trail (14–16). There are numerous other instances of animal imagery applied to humans,[10] and the Joads are subject, like other animals, to the natural elements, from the dust storms at the beginning to the deluge at the end of the novel. Michael K is associated by the narrator, by himself, and by other characters with a variety of creatures: a snail (3), an ant (83, 97), a worm (107, 182), a parasite (116), a stick insect (149), a coelacanth (151), a dog (30), a rabbit (39, 164), a beast (40), an owl (56), a lizard (114, 139), a duckling (142), a budgie, a mouse, a monkey (181), and a mole (182). At one point the narrator says that Michael can sense poisonous plants, "as though he had once been an animal and the knowledge of good and bad plants had not died in his soul" (102). Coetzee clearly wishes his gardener to be perceived in naturalistic terms, as a creature of the earth.

The earth itself figures as a protean element in each novel, at times barren and abused, at others nurtured and fruitful, but always enduring. In each work, there are those who are indifferent to the welfare of the earth and those who recognize it as a source of life. In his essay on the farm novel, Coetzee points out that "in the United States, where land has been plentiful and where there was never a native peasantry, the dynamics of pastoralism have been different, turning on the question of whether the farmer should treat the land as a nurturing mother or object of rape" (75). Steinbeck's bankers and large landholders fall into the latter category, seeing the land only in terms of profit, as an object to be exploited. Similarly, the South African government troops, as well as the rebel guerrillas who bivouac in the fields where Michael has painstakingly nurtured his pumpkins are insensible to the damage to the earth caused by themselves and their donkeys. Michael finds his plants' vines trampled and cropped: "There were long severed creepers winding through the grass whose leaves were already furling and drooping; the few kernels that had shot, little green nuts no bigger than marbles, were devoured" (111). The troops improvidently squander the water that Michael has so carefully conserved, allowing it to flood the fields: "That is a mistake, thought K, that is a sign" (111). The government troops who arrest K at the end of part 1 are even more destructive of the earth. After cutting and tossing Michael's pumpkins in a pile, they dig in the same earth to plant their crop, land mines, to prepare a harvest of death for whoever may step there.

Both Steinbeck and Coetzee stress the wastage and spoilage which inevitably results from an indifferent or destructive attitude toward the earth. In California of the Depression, surplus crops and the profit motive lead to the abandonment or destruction of food while people die of malnutrition: "And the yellow fruit falls heavily to the ground and . . . yellow jackets dig into the soft meat, and there is a smell of ferment and rot. . . . The decay spreads over the State, and the sweet smell is a great sorrow on the land" (384). Coetzee employs similar images. While on the road to the farm, Michael, dizzy with hunger, climbs through a barbed-wire fence into "an apple orchard overgrown with grass and weeds. Worm-eaten fruit lay everywhere underfoot; the fruit on the branches was undersized and infested. . . . He moved deeper into the orchard. Everywhere was evidence of neglect" (39). In this South African setting, the cause of wastage within fenced lands seems to be the result, not of a profit motive, but of indifference. Michael at first thinks this land must be abandoned, but when he looks beyond the orchard, he sees an apparently prosperous and well-tended farmhouse and fields.

The problem that both Steinbeck and Coetzee confront is that the dispossessed who would care for the land are fenced out by those who own. Steinbeck's uprooted farmers, working for the big growers at penurious wages, attempt to plant private patches, "Secret gardens hidden in the weeds. A package of carrot seeds and a few turnips. Planted potato skins, crept out in the evening secretly to hoe in the stolen earth" (259). Their efforts are in vain, for all of the land is owned, and even to plant the land left in weeds is trespassing.

Michael K's experience in the vastness of South Africa is much the same: "He could understand that people should have retreated here and fenced themselves in with miles and miles of silence . . . (though by what right he was not sure); he wondered whether there were not forgotten corners and angles and corridors between the fences, land that belonged to no one yet" (47). He thinks he has found such a place when he reaches the abandoned Visagie farm, which seems to be inhabited only by wild animals and where nothing grows in the garden. Filled with a sense of "exultation . . . that he, alone and unknown, was making this deserted farm bloom" (59), he scatters his mother's ashes on the earth, restores the dam, and plants his seeds. A short time later he is confronted by a pale plump young man who introduces himself as "boss Visagie's grandson" (60). K reflects, "I let myself believe that this was one of those islands without an owner. Now I am learning the truth. Now I am learning my lesson" (61). In a 1983 interview, Coetzee pointed out that Michael "can't hope to keep the garden because, finally, the whole surface of South Africa has been surveyed and mapped and disposed of" (Morphet interview, 456).

Nevertheless, Michael K pursues his plan of becoming a secret gardener. He literally becomes a child of the earth, building his burrow where "two low hills, like plump breasts, curved toward each other" (100). He seeds, waters, and tends to his plants by night, thinking of them as his "children" (101), the melons "two sisters," the pumpkins "a band of brothers" (113). He becomes a "tender of the soil" (113) and understands the idea "From one seed a whole handful: that was what it meant to say *the bounty of the earth*" (118). He knows what the soldiers on both sides and many of the owners do not know: "there must be men to stay behind and keep gardening alive, or at least the idea of gardening; because once that cord was broken, the earth would grow hard and forget her children. That was why" (109). And he knows, as Whitman knew, that ultimately all living things are one with the earth:

"There will be not a grain left bearing my marks, just as my mother has now, after her season in the earth, been washed clean, blown about, and drawn up into the leaves of grass" (124).

Steinbeck and Coetzee both end their novels with a reminder that the earth endures, life endures. In Southern California, "Tiny points of grass came through the earth, and in a few days the hills were pale green with the beginning year" (480). And in South Africa, Michael K remembers "the mountains purple and pink in the distance . . . the earth grey and brown beneath the sun save here and there, where if you looked carefully you suddenly saw a tip of vivid green, pumpkin leaf or carrot-bush" (183).

While *Life and Times of Michael K* clearly has correspondences to the naturalistic agrarian-protest novel and *The Grapes of Wrath* specifically, it is also in certain respects a subversion of the genre. The wrath, anger, and political activism espoused by Steinbeck as necessary elements in the struggle become in Coetzee's novel Michael's silent disapproval and passive resistance. In Steinbeck's work there is a pervasive sense of an ultimate unity of the migrants, a realization of a bonding, the movement from "I to we." This unifying element is left much more problematical at the conclusion of Coetzee's novel, as we shall see.

THE DOCTOR'S DILEMMA

Part 2 of the novel is set near Cape Town in a former horse racing track that has been converted into a rehabilitation camp for captured rebels. After being arrested at the farm as a suspected rebel at the end of part 1, Michael, near starvation, is an object of both imprisonment and charity as a patient in the hospital attached to the camp. In this brief second section (which comprises only about 20 percent of the novel), Coetzee shifts the narrative point of view to the first-person account of a "pharmacist turned makeshift medical officer" (162) who tends to and becomes obsessed with Michael K. This shift in point of view will be examined after we have discussed the nature of the medical officer.

As a representative of Empire, colonialism, and white South Africans, the officer is disillusioned in the extreme. He sees the end purpose of his work in the hospital as absurd. His task is to nurture patients like Michael back to health, he observes, "so that one day soon he can rejoin camp life and have a chance to march back and forth across the racetrack and shout slogans and salute the flag and practice digging holes and filling them up again" (133). He asks, "Do any of us believe in what we are doing here? I doubt it" (134). His commanding officer, ironically named Nöel, although similarly disenchanted, can at least remember their official purpose: "We are fighting this war . . . so that minorities will have a say in their destinies" (157)—minorities referring to South African whites. The medical officer hopes that the remote authorities in "the Castle" (152) will forget about them, but in the meantime, like some fugitive from a Beckett play, he has the overpowering conviction "that I was wasting my life, that I was wasting it by living from day to day in a state of waiting" (157). Coetzee forecasts a grim future for the Afrikaner cause as the already overtaxed medical staff receives a shipment of four hundred new patients, many of them in "a state of life in death or death in life" (159).

The medical officer's attitude toward Michael (whom he and Nöel insist on regarding as a plurality, "Michaels") is, like that of many white South Africans toward their nonwhite countrymen, filled with contradictions. His shifting views of Michael K cover a spectrum ranging from compassion, to condescension and paternalism, to hostility, ending finally in idealization. Michael's emaciated state stirs the officer's compassion as he tries to nurse him back to health; he also offers to surgically correct his harelip. When Michael refuses both offers, the officer concludes that perhaps Michael "only eats the bread of freedom" (146), and he buys him food that Michael relishes, a squash, near relative of the pumpkin. He also tries to persuade Nöel to release Michael and eventually ends the force-feeding, concluding that Michael must be free.

The officer's compassion, however, is easily displaced by his feelings of condescension, as when he regards Michael as "but one of a multitude of the second class" (136), or when he tells Nöel that Michael is "a simpleton, and not even an interesting simpleton" (141), although his motive here may be to protect Michael from being interrogated. His paternalistic attitude is evidenced when the officer proclaims, "I am the only one who can save you" (151), coupled with the command, "*yield!*" (152).

A compassion that is grounded in condescension finds its way easily enough to hostile domination. Exasperated by Michael's refusal to provide information, the officer resorts to threats: "You are going to learn to fill sandbags and dig holes, my friend, till your back breaks! . . . and if you don't survive, tough luck" (138). At one point he regards Michael as an "albatross about my neck" (146) and decides, "It would have been better if his mother had quietly suffocated him when she saw what he was, and put him in a trash can" (155).

This consciousness which can view Michael at one moment as garbage, can change, chameleonlike, and see him next as a "prodigy" (142), as "a human soul above and beneath classification, a soul blessedly untouched by doctrine, untouched by history" (151). Toward the end of his narrative, the medical officer apotheosizes his unyielding patient in an imaginary supplication: "Michaels, forgive me for the way I treated you, I did not appreciate who you were until the last days. Forgive me too for following you like this. I promise not to be a burden. . . . I have chosen you to show me the way" (162–63). Finally, he speaks of Michael's "sacred and alluring garden that blooms in the heart of the desert and produces the food of life" (166).

Coetzee's inclusion of the medical officer's narrative in part 2 has prompted critical discussion in two areas: the appropriateness of shifting the point of view, and the nature of the officer's character. Teresa Dovey has pointed out that the primary narrator of parts 1 and 3 often employs "free indirect speech, which combines the voice of narrator and character" (*Novels*, 282), so that the two are in many instances indistinguishable. Coetzee's bonding of these two voices is so seamless, that his shift in the second section is rather jarring, as several early reviewers noted. One reviewer, however, praised the change in point of view for providing an "objective look at K," but felt that the change was compromised by a return in part 3 to the original narrator: "when Coetzee switches back at the end [to] K's point of view, the credibility is broken. It made me wish the doctor *had* followed K to the bitter end, or that the alternative viewpoint had never been used in the first place." [11] Another critic argues: "Without the second and third parts of the book the full message of K's freedom may not have been understood." [12]

Having found the narrative change in part 2 rather abrupt myself, I asked Coetzee about this matter in the writers' workshop in Lexington:

Penner: To go back to point of view, in *Michael K* you make this sudden shift, from an omniscient narrator to the medical officer. Could you tell us how you came to make that decision, to get out of Michael's point of view and into this other?

Coetzee: It is simply a decision that the novel, part 1—which is up to the point that you are talking about—wasn't substantial enough; that it was actually just, you know, a year and a bit in a guy's life, and that if it had gone on like that, it would have been a narrative of two years of a guy's life.

Penner: Is it because Michael's consciousness is limited and you wanted to have someone out of the Empire, so to speak?

Coetzee: Yes.

Stephen Watson sees the medical officer as a representative of Empire, including him among those "colonizers who wish to elude at almost any cost their historical roles as colonizers" and who wish to escape "the intolerable burdens of the master/slave relationship" ("Colonialism," 378). Although we are not given Michael's thoughts in this section, we may surmise that he refuses the medical officer's treatment because he sees behind the mask of kindness of the old master/slave relationship which will require him to "*yield*," as the officer says. [13] On the other hand, Coetzee has defended the officer's character: "He heals people, he helps people, he protects people. Does it matter that his actions don't satisfy him? Maybe the world would be a better place if there were more people like him around. Maybe. I put the question, anyhow" (Morphet interview, 457).

The dissatisfaction that some readers have with part 2 probably has less to do with the officer's character or the shift in point of view (which happens repeatedly in *Dusklands* and again at the end of *Foe*), than with the relation of this segment to the rest of the work. After having our imaginations intrigued for most of the novel with the evolving consciousness of Michael K and with his familial relationship with the earth and his "children," we are suddenly required to shift our attention to a character whose monologue is self-contradictory and magniloquent, "the over-insistent ruminations of the medical officer."[14] This segment is perhaps best viewed as an aesthetic choice which did not work as well as it might have, one which is a consequence of Coetzee's feeling a necessity to include a point of view other than Michael K's.

SEEDS

The brief final section of the novel is a return to the beginning: to Cape Town, briefly to the room where Michael's mother lived, but mostly to nearby Sea Point, which Coetzee described in our interview as "a sort of—how shall I say—a Miami Beach of South Africa, a bit maybe toned down, but yeah, there are a lot of street walkers and there's this strange mixture of wealthy apartment life and seedy street life going on at the same time." The Sea Point which Michael K finds in Coetzee's projection of the "nearer future" of South Africa is an incongruous mixture of holiday atmosphere amid the rubble of war: burnt-out cars and buildings, an ice-cream vendor, "a trio of girls in shorts and singlets . . . leaving a sweet smell in their wake" (171).

Michael's experiences in this segment have an aura of sad sordidness about them. He is taken up by two pimps and their whores, to whom the emaciated and inarticulate Michael is a diversion. One of the pimps insists that he drink wine and brandy, which causes Michael to vomit and get dizzy. One of the prostitutes seduces him, after which he feels shame. The effect of this, as one critic puts it, is that "K becomes the derelict so familiar to South African eyes. . . . This is a Michael K we can recognize, the type of non-person we are used to closing our consciences to."[15] Coetzee gives this explanation for including these events in Michael's life: "It is important that K should not emerge from the book as an angel" (Morphet interview, 457). Michael emerges, rather, as a credible human being who reflects, after the departure of the whores and pimps, "I have become an object of charity. . . . Everywhere I go there are people waiting to exercise their forms of charity on me" (181).

More important, however, is Michael's realization that he has found his essence: "the truth is that I have been a gardener. . . . *The truth, the truth about me. 'I am a gardener'* " (181). His story ends with Michael imagining conditions under which he can succeed as a gardener, the primary condition being to have "plenty of seeds, a different packet of seeds for each pocket: pumpkin seeds, marrow seeds, beans, carrot seeds, beet-root seeds. . . . Seeds in my shoes too, and in the lining of my coat" (182). He envisions his future as a gardener, not in solitude, but in companionship, imagining "a little old man with a stoop" with whom he could share a bed and for whom he could obtain water from the demolished pumps with a teaspoon and a string, saying with his closing words, "in that way . . . one can live" (184).

Life and Times of Michael K is an almost unqualified artistic success. Aside from the medical officer's narrative, Coetzee has produced an unforgettable portrait of war-torn South Africa and Michael's evolving consciousness and sense of being. He has also, I believe, successfully adapted the traditional farm and agrarian-protest novel to his purposes, evoking Michael K's bonding to the earth and its harvest.

By the time one reaches the end of Michael K's journey, Coetzee's epigraph from Heraclitus still remains puzzling:

> War is the father of all and king of all.
> Some he shows as gods, others as men.
> Some he makes slaves, and others free.

Portions of the commentary on this fragment by classical scholar G. S. Kirk (credited in Coetzee's acknowledgments) are helpful. Setting aside the question of gods and kings, who hold no sinecure in Coetzee's cosmos, we can ascribe to war not only its specific meaning, but as well the broader sense of strife, the "interaction of opposites" inherent in being.[16] Michael K is not a god or king, but a man, who has clung to his freedom, like a plant to soil, against all odds. André Brink provides a fitting conclusion: "Michael K does not merely contemplate the world; he produces meaning through his existence; in the final analysis he becomes meaning."[17]

NOTES

1. Robert Post, "Oppression in the Fiction of J. M. Coetzee," *Critique* 27, no. 2 (1986): 67.

2. Nadine Gordimer, "The Idea of Gardening," *New York Review of Books*, 2 February 1984, 3.

3. Teresa Dovey, *The Novels of J. M. Coetzee: Lacanian Allegories*, Human Sciences Research Council Publication Series, no. 86 (Johannesburg: Ad. Donker, 1988), 11.

    4. Interview with Tony Morphet, "Two Interviews with J. M. Coetzee, 1983 and 1987," *From South Africa*, spec. issue of *TriQuarterly* (Evanston: Northwestern Univ. Press, 1987): 457.

    5. Franz Kafka, "A Hunger Artist," *The Penal Colony*, translated by Willa and Edwin Muir (New York: Schocken Books, 1961), 255.

    6. Lao-Tsu, *Tao Te Ching*, translated by Gia-Fu Feng and Jane English (New York: Random House, 1972): sec. 43, 56.

    7. Stephen Watson, "Colonialism in the Novels of J. M. Coetzee," *Research in African Literatures*: 17 (1986): 378.

    8. J. M. Coetzee, "Idleness in South Africa," *Social Dynamics* 8 (1982): 1–13; "Pauline Smith and the Afrikaans Language," *English in Africa* 8, no. 1 (1981): 25–32; "Lineal Consciousness in the Farm Novels of C. M. van den Heever," Assn. of University English Teachers of South Africa Conference, Cape Town (July 1985): 3–5; "Farm Novel and *Plaasroman*," in *White Writing* (New Haven and London: Yale Univ. Press, 1988), 63–81; an earlier version appeared under the title "Farm Novel and *Plaasroman* in South Africa," *English in Africa* 13, no. 2 (1986): 1–19.

    9. John Steinbeck, *The Grapes of Wrath* (New York: Viking-Bantam, 1971); all references are to this edition.

    10. See, for example, Robert J. Griffin and William A. Freedman, "Machines and Animals: Pervasive Motifs in *The Grapes of Wrath*," in *John Steinbeck, The Grapes of Wrath, Text and Criticism*, edited by Peter Lisca (New York: Penguin, 1977), 769–83.

    11. Dean Flower, "Fiction Chronicle," *Hudson Review* 37, no. 2. (Summer 1984): 314.

    12. Helene Müller, "Who Is Michael K?" *Standpunte* 38, no. 1 (February 1985): 43.

    13. Linda Norton, my former student, in an unpublished paper, "Analysis of Michael K."

    14. D. J. Enright, "The Thing Itself," *Times Literary Supplement* (London: 30 September 1983): 1035.

    15. Müller, "Who Is Michael K?" 43.

    16. Heraclitus, *The Cosmic Fragments*, edited by G. S. Kirk (Cambridge: Cambridge Univ. Press, 1954), 249.

    17. André Brink, "Writing Against Big Brother: Notes on Apocalyptic Fiction in South Africa," *World Literature Today* 58, no. 2 (1984): 194.

7

Foe: The Absurd, the Muse, and the Colonial Dilemma

TWICE-TOLD TALES

Coetzee's fifth novel is a mélange: a retelling of *Robinson Crusoe* with Absurdist overtones, a commentary on the art of fiction, and an analogue of South Africa's political and racial dilemmas. *Foe* provides the proper ingredients to recreate the adventure and pleasure of the eighteenth-century travel genre from which it is partially derived—the urgency of survival, mutinies, piracies, the abducted child, the castaway, the rumored cannibal—but in place of the eighteenth century's obligatory moralizing, there is our own era's passion for the self-reflexive narrative, the modern novel self-consciously appropriating the form of its forebearers, the novel commenting on the nature of the novel, art reflecting on art. As Michiko Kakutani has pointed out in a review of *Foe*, "the operative forces are not so much history or politics as art and imagination—how can one individual's story be apprehended and translated through language by another?" [1]

This engaging revision of the story Defoe told is told again by the castaway narrator Coetzee conceived, the imaginative and resourceful Susan Barton, "a tall woman with black hair and dark eyes" (86). Barton is at once as resilient and opportunistic as Defoe's Moll Flanders, and as sensual and as creatively observant as Joyce Cary's Sara Monday. Her enlivening spirit creates a narrative tone quite distinct from Coetzee's earlier works.

By her own account, she was raised in England, descended from a French father and an English mother. Two years before her narrative begins, she had traveled to Bahia (now Salvador, Brazil) in search of her only daughter, who had been abducted by an English factor. Her search coming to naught, she embarked for Lisbon on a merchantman, whose crew mutinied within ten days. Barton and the corpse of the captain (her former lover; now with a handspike in one eye) are cast adrift, which brings us to the opening line of the novel: "At last I could row no further" (5). Abandoning the dinghy and the corpse, she swims ashore, "my long hair floating about me, like a flower of the sea, like an anemone," and lies sprawled on the sand under the "orange blaze of the sun . . . tired, grateful, like all the saved" (5).

The Cruso (as Coetzee spells his name) that Susan Barton encounters on the island resembles Defoe's adventurer only in externals: in the sun-bleached hair and shaggy beard, the rough jerkin, cone-shaped cap, and sturdy sandals, all made of pelts. There similarities end. Defoe's Crusoe as a young man is a restless adventurer who tries his hand as a Brazilian plantation owner and slave trader before destiny casts him up on his island. There he proves to be an ordinary, but resourceful man, in extraordinary circumstances. Through self-assertion, his belief in his Protestant God, and Reason, he overcomes Nature and a tendency to despair. Crusoe sees in his circumstance a divine purpose: to subdue the savages and civilize the island. He regards his survival as a result of both Providence and his own endeavor. For example, God causes some castaway seeds of corn to sprout, but it is Crusoe who husbands the earth and saves each crop of seeds for the next four years. He fails at making a wooden cask, but succeeds at bringing provisions from the ship, building a fort, making tools, hewing logs, teaching a parrot to speak, domesticating wild goats, making a goat-skin umbrella, and, when visitors arrive, establishing a community with religious freedom. He regards himself as "lord of the whole manor . . . king, or emperor over the whole country."[2] It never occurs to him not to keep a journal, only how to conserve his ink for the most important events. At the end of his twenty-eight years on the island, Defoe's Crusoe is still an adventurous and energetic man.

Coetzee's Cruso has little of the vigor and none of the optimism of Defoe's character. His forebearers are more likely to be found roaming Beckett's bleak landscapes of the Absurd than on the highways or sea-lanes of any eighteenth-century novel. At age sixty, Cruso has settled into somber stolidity, grudging of his energy and his attention. He had once bestirred himself to construct a well-made hut, fence, gate, and oven, but his efforts beyond that are a study in minimalism: for agriculture, a patch of wild bitter lettuce, for furniture, a narrow bed. Barton observes that he has kept no record of the passing time, and no journal, because, she believes, "he lacked the inclination to keep one, or, if he ever possessed the inclination, had lost it" (16). Cruso rejects Barton's suggestion that he keep a journal, saying, "Nothing is forgotten. . . . Nothing I have forgotten is worth the remembering" (17). Had he kept a journal, it would have been unreliable, Barton con-

cludes; for he tells her one day that he is the son of a wealthy mer-
chant, the next 'a poor lad with no family; one day that Friday had
arrived as "a mere child, a little slave boy," the next that Friday had
been an adult cannibal whom Cruso had saved from being roasted (12).
Obviously "truth" is a matter of complete indifference to Cruso.

Barton is vexed by yet another trait—his inflexible refusal to indulge
in "progress." When she suggests that they make some candles, he re-
torts that it is easier to learn to see in the dark; when she proposes
diving for tools in the wrecked ship (he has never bothered) Cruso
replies that salt and seaworms would have done for the tools, and any-
way, "We sleep, we eat, we live. We have no need of tools" (32).

The one activity that does engage his imagination and his energy
arises straight from the annals of the Absurd. For years Cruso and
Friday have labored to construct massive stone terraces, now twelve in
number, the stone walls "a yard thick and at their highest as high as a
man's head" (33). This structure is comprised of a hundred thousand
or more stones, the earth between the walls cleared and leveled. When
practical-minded Susan asks what is to be planted in this monumental
edifice, Cruso replies with "sorry dignity," "We have nothing to plant—
that is our misfortune. . . . The planting is reserved for those who
come after us and have the foresight to bring seed" (33). Thus Cruso
is, from Barton's view, a willing Sisyphus, a barren Demeter. But for
him the endeavor represents a journal without words: "I will leave behind my terraces and walls. . . . They will be enough. They will be
more than enough" (18). Obviously, Cruso is at the furthest extreme
from the nurturing gardener Michael K; he is more akin to Magda in
his relation to stones.

Coetzee's Friday is also a striking contrast to Defoe's, a Carib whom
Crusoe described as "a comely, handsome fellow, perfectly well made,
with straight strong limbs, not too large, tall and well-shaped . . . and
a great vivacity and sparkling sharpness in his eyes. . . . His skin was
not quite black, but very tawny . . . of a bright kind of dun olive colour
that had in it something very agreeable" (202). Susan Barton's perception of Coetzee's latter-day Friday, an African, is quite negative: "the
small dull eyes, the broad nose, the thick lips, the skin not black but a
dark grey, dry as if coated with dust" (6). She observes more than once
that she finds Friday "in all matters a dull fellow" (22).

Defoe's pragmatic Crusoe initially taught Friday the only three words
requisite for an obedient servant/slave: "Master, yes, and no," although
Friday later developed a pigdin English which Defoe used for comic
effect. Even with his limited verbal skills, Defoe's Friday had a penchant for asking ingenuous questions to probe Crusoe's Protestant soul:
"if God much strong, much might as the Devil, why God no kill the
Devil, so make him no more do wicked?" (214–15). Defoe's Friday was

as well a bold-spirited, good-natured fellow who could laugh in the face of danger, as he demonstrated in his daredevil antics with a wild bear, which, at great risk, he lured up a tree and out onto a slender limb, from which Friday then dropped neatly to safety. While Crusoe never forgets the gulf between master and servant, he can say, "I began really to love the creature; and on his side, I believed he loved me more than it was possible for him ever to love anything before" (210).

Coetzee has drawn his Friday as a speechless but gentler Caliban, a sullen, solitary, enigmatic mute, his tongue having been cut out, Cruso claims, by slavers. Barton speculates that Cruso himself may have severed Friday's tongue, but the question is never answered. Like his predecessor, this slave is obedient in all things to his master. However, the inaccessible silence of Coetzee's Friday forces our attention on his masters, first Cruso, then Barton. Aside from the terraces, Cruso manifests little interest in anything or anyone, including Friday. When Barton asks Cruso how many words he has taught Friday, he replies tersely, "As many as he needs" (21). Thus, Friday knows the functional word *firewood*, which he fetches, but does not know the broader category *wood*. While Cruso does not abuse Friday, he never seems to regard him as more than a fetcher of wood, a catcher of fish, one who can hum in a low tongueless register, "The voice of man," as Cruso says (22).

If Cruso and Friday are but grim shades of their eighteenth-century originals, Susan Barton embodies the spirit of the heroes and heroines who brought to life the pages of Defoe, Fielding, Smollett, and Sterne (Richardson's "virtue" is another matter). While there are many facets to her personality, her essence is that she is a teller of tales, and as such, she carries the central theme of Coetzee's *Foe*, the nature of narrative art.

FICTION'S FABRIC

Amazed that Cruso has kept no journal, Barton attempts to prompt his recollections of his first emotions when he was cast upon the island, a vivid element in Defoe's novel. She asks, "What memories do you even now preserve of the fatal storm, the prayers of your companions, your terror when the waves engulfed you, your gratitude as you were cast up on the shore, your fear of savage beasts, the discomforts of those first nights . . . ?" (17). Moreover, like the eighteenth-century masters and any good fictionist, Barton knows that verisimilitude owes much to "particularity": those "thousand touches which today may seem of no importance. . . . When you made your needle (the needle you store in your belt) by what means did you pierce the eye? When you sewed your hat, what did you use for thread? Touches like these will one day persuade your countrymen that it is all true, every word" (18). Such advice, of course, is a matter of indifference to Cruso.

Barton is as little able to fire his creative imagination as she is his sexual passion. They make love only once after his fifteen years of celibacy, and it is apparently enough for him, for he never raises the subject again. She perceives correctly, "the idea of a Cruso on his island is a better thing than the true Cruso tight-lipped and sullen" (35). This foreshadows Cruso's end. After the three castaways are rescued by the crew of the *John Hobart*, Cruso's health begins to fail, despite Susan's attempts to revive him by "swimming" on his body, and he dies of "extremist woe" (43) three days before the ship makes port in Bristol. Undaunted, Barton knows that she alone has "disposal of all that Cruso leaves behind, which is the story of his island" (45).

Transforming experience into fiction is not a simple task, Coetzee suggests. When the captain of the *John Hobart* encourages Barton to sell the tale to booksellers, she replies, "A liveliness is lost in the writing down which must be supplied by art, and I have no art" (40). The well-meaning captain assures her that "the booksellers will hire a man to set your story to rights, and put in a dash of color too, here and there." Barton responds that she "will not have any lies told," which causes the captain to smile, saying, "their trade is in books, not in truth" (40). As though anticipating the bizarre conclusion of *Foe*, Barton reflects, "I might as well have dreamed it" (40).

As the first section of the novel ends, we are informed that all we have read thus far has been an epistolary journal written by Barton to a "Mr. Foe," Defoe's surname at birth. Teresa Dovey observes that Foe, as the person to whom Barton's numerous correspondences are addressed, is "the Other, or the *sujet supposé savoir*, whose response, it is hoped, will constitute the truth of the speaking subject."[3] Since no written responses from Foe are given, Barton must look elsewhere for confirmation of the truth of her being.

From this point on, it is impossible to tell whether the events Barton relates really "happen" or if they are dreamed or imagined, recalling Coetzee's earlier blurring of "reality" in *In the Heart of the Country*. Barton's penned request to Foe—"Can you not take us into your house?" (49)—is apparently immediately followed by the accomplished fact, with a host of "particularities." Barton perceives Foe writing with a rug over his knees, pantoufles on his feet; in the mornings he wipes mouse-droppings from the table. Coetzee, through Barton, brushes on the canvas the seemingly incidental visual touches that are requisite to memorable writing: "There is a ripple in the window-pane. Moving your head, you can make the ripple travel over the cows grazing in the pasture, over the plowed land beyond, over the line of poplars, and up into the sky" (50).

Barton soon begins to doubt the substantiality of her experiences, her story, and herself. She questions how she reached Bahia and how she survived there for two years; and then she turns the experience into a metaphor of solitariness: "Was Bahia an island in the ocean of the Brazilian forest, and my room a lonely island in Bahia?" The murdered captain becomes a mythic figure (foreshadowing the conclusion), fated "to drift forever in the southernmost seas, clothed in ice" (51). In seeming desperation, she implores Foe, "Return to me the substance I have lost," by using his conjurer's craft to see waves when there are fields before him, to feel a torrid sun in winter.

PAPER ISLANDS, STONE WORDS

Barton recognizes the insubstantiality of reality, the permanence of art. She imagines the alterations taking place on the island: her body's imprint on the grass bed growing fainter each day, the wind erasing her footprints and picking at the thatched roof of the hut. Only the walls and terraces will remain, and they will be misunderstood by later visitors: "they will say, 'These are cannibal walls, the ruins of a cannibal city, from the golden age of cannibals'" (54–55). Until a reality, even a reality embroidered with colorful lies, is fixed in the durable pigments of words, it is protean, shifting, vanishing. To underscore this, Coetzee echoes a scene in the first self-reflexive novel of all, *Don Quixote*, where, in part 2, the Knight of la Mancha and his earthy squire debate passages from the previously published part 1 of their exploits. Similarly, Barton tells an uncomprehending Friday that she will give him his "own copy of our book, bound in leather. . . . Are you not filled with joy to know that you will live forever, after a manner?" (58).

Susan Barton's earlier imagined presence of Foe dissolves into his real (or imagined) absence. Apparently he has gone into hiding from his creditors while Susan and Friday occupy his vacant house in Clock Lane off Long Acres (47), posing as cook and gardener. Susan supplies their frugal needs by occasionally selling furnishings from the house while occupying her time talking to a mute and presumably uncomprehending Friday and writing long, unanswered letters to Foe. When the letters return unopened, she continues to write to him, tossing the letters in a trunk. Here the momentum of the novel begins to falter as theories of narrative displace event.

Barton's principal concern in this one-way correspondence involves the relation of fiction to life. Revising her earlier insistence to the captain of the *John Hobart* on the primacy of truth in art, she now accepts the truism that "what we can accept in life we cannot accept in history" (67), apparently in Henry Fielding's sense of prose fiction or the epic in prose as "history."[4] Thus, she asks, who would want to read the truth, "that there were once two dull fellows on a rock in the sea who filled their time by digging up stones?" (82). Barton reasons that the writer must find mystery in the mundane and that the principal mysteries of the island are five:

1. The terraces: Would Cruso and Friday not have been "as fruitfully occupied in watering the stones where they lay and waiting for them to sprout?" (83)

2. The missing tongue: Did Cruso himself sever it and blame the slavers? The tongue, with which we "jest and lie and seduce" is one of the "members of play" which raises us above the beasts (85). Does this explain Friday's sullen nature?

3. Friday's submission: Why did he not revolt and slay Cruso as he slept? "Is there something in the condition of slavehood that invades the heart and makes a slave a slave for life?" (85), echoing Magda's earlier thoughts on the subject.

4. Failed desire: Why did neither Friday nor Cruso desire her? Did "Cruso in his way and do you [Friday] in your way believe I came to claim dominion over you?" (86)

5. Friday's ritual: Why did Friday scatter white flower petals in the water above the place where the ship that carried him sank? Barton believes it was in memory of someone who perished, but other explanations are given later.

Barton pursues these mysteries, she explains to Friday, "because they are the questions any reader of our story will ask" (86).

Acting as her own taskmaster, Barton attempts to explain to Friday her plight as a writer through an analogy: the paper is an island, and the words are stones which must be repeatedly dispersed day after day according to varying schemes. She is a slave to her task as Friday was to Cruso, and hers is particularly hard because Cruso and Friday lacked desire (which Magda saw as intrinsic to life): "Without desire how is it possible to make a story?" (88). Easier to build a story on the sorrows of Friday, she reflects, than on the indifference of Cruso. But it is the writer's task to transform a dull subject through the creative imagination, by highlighting colors, casting light against shadow, teasing from episodes "their hidden meanings, braiding these together as one braids rope" (89). The ability to select the appropriate episodes is called the art of divining, or "the grace of illumination" (89). (Barton's anguish with her task is paralleled by remarks Coetzee made in an interview in 1978: "I don't like writing and have to push myself. . . . It's far from compulsion. It's bad if I do write and worse if I don't" ["Speaking," 21].) Barton ends her solitary discourse on a note of desperation: "Dear Mr. Foe, I am growing to understand why you wanted Cruso to have a musket and be besieged by cannibals. . . . You are a writer who knows above all how many words can be sucked from a cannibal feast, how few from a woman cowering in the wind. It is all a matter of words and numbers of words, is it not?" (94).

TWO AUTHORS IN SEARCH OF A MUSE

In part 3, Barton sets out on the road with the purpose of finding Friday safe passage to Africa; failing that, the two locate Foe in his Whitechapel hideaway (113). Her former monologue now evolves into a dialectic with Foe over aesthetics. Foe, as a professional writer mindful of his public's tastes and the booksellers' profits, argues that the island story provides "novelty" but that it is not a story in itself; it is nourishing, like a loaf of bread, but inherently uninteresting, for it lacks "light and shade" (117). It will do as part of a larger story, which Foe breaks into five parts: (1) the lost daughter, (2) the mother's quest for the daughter in Bahia, (3) the island, (4) the daughter's quest for the mother, and (5) reunion in England. "It is thus that we make up a book," Foe instructs: "loss, then quest, then recovery; beginning, then middle, then end" (117).

This is neat, but not neat enough for Barton, who counters with her own triptych: (1) the story of how she came to be marooned (told by Barton to Cruso), (2) the story of Cruso's shipwreck and early years on the island (told by Cruso to Barton), and (3) the story of Friday, which she says is "properly not a story but a puzzle or hole in the narrative" (121). Susan acknowledges that her narrative plan has a weakness in the middle section where Cruso spent too much time building terraces and she too much time tramping the shores; however, she rejects Foe's invention of cannibals and pirates, "because they were not the truth," as she rejects his lost daughter story.

Despite Barton's reservations, Coetzee introduces an Absurdist lost daughter subplot, apparently stage-managed by Foe, but springing from the brow of Pirandello's *Six Characters in Search of an Author*. In part 2, while Barton and Friday are staying at Foe's house at Clock Lane, a strange young woman appears who claims that she, too, is named Susan Barton, and that she is Barton's daughter. This improbable plant, Barton surmises, has been concocted by Foe to make his fiction come to life and to persuade her of its validity. To Barton, the stratagem is a shabby subterfuge shot through with inconsistencies. The elements of the girl's story have been the stock in trade of romances for centuries: she says that her father was an improvident brewer and gambler named George Lewes (Barton points out the discrepancy in names) who fled his creditors and is rumored to have perished in the Low Countries. The girl is then left with her destitute mother and a servant named Emmy or Amy (shades of Defoe's *Roxanna*). In desperation, the mother abandons the child, who is stolen and raised by Gypsies. The girl attempts the traditional recognition scene by saying that her mother's hands and eyes are identical to hers. Barton observes that her hands and the girl's are nothing alike, that the girl's eyes are grey (later blue) (132), while Barton's are brown, that the girl's hair is hazel-brown, Barton's black. To refute this improbable story, Barton appeals to the authority of fictional tradition: it is "only in books that children are stolen by gipsies [sic]" (78) and while there are many stories of mothers searching for lost daughters "there are no stories of daughters searching for mothers" (77). Thus, to be plausible, life must imitate art.

After the girl reveals that she knows the stories of Bahia and the island, Barton in a dream takes her on a journey in "the darkest part of the forest" to find her "real mother." There she tells the girl, "What you know of your parentage comes to you in the form of stories, and the stories have but a single source," who is, of course, Daniel Foe: "You are father-born. You have no mother" (91). Later, after Barton and Friday arrive at Foe's Whitechapel hideaway, the "daughter" reappears, bringing in tow a woman she claims is her childhood nurse, Amy.

At this point, like some Pirandellan character in search not of an author, but of her own ontology, Barton challenges Foe, accusing him of running a "gathering-place of actors" who will claim that she is but an actor too. She demands, "how can we live if we do not believe we know who we are, and who we have been?" (130). She refuses to be a receptacle for whatever tale is stuffed into her and thus become a "house of words, hollow, without substance" (as Magda felt). Rather, she will be "a free woman who asserts her freedom by telling her story according to her own desire" (131). Uncertainty assails her, however. If the girl and Amy are Foe's creations, then who is Barton and who is Foe? "all my life grows to be story and. . . . Nothing is left to me but doubt. I am doubt itself. Who is speaking to me? Am I a phantom too? . . . And you: who are you?" (133).

Foe's response is to take her in his arms and kiss her and give her a Nabokovian reassurance that only what is imagined is real. If we have been called into the world from a "different order," now forgotten, by a conjurer, "have we thereby lost our freedom? . . . Do we of necessity become puppets in a story whose end is invisible to us . . . ?" (135). No, Foe concludes, for writing and conjuring (and we may infer, life) are much the same: a cloud shaped like a camel floats by, and our fantasy takes us to Africa; a new cloud in the form of a sailing-ship appears, and we are transported to a desert isle. "Have we cause to believe that the lives it is given us to live proceed with any more design than these whimsical adventures?" (135). The synthesis of their dialectic is that these two creations by Coetzee, Barton, and Foe, slip into bed with each other to see if they cannot create some pleasurable issue, fictional or otherwise. Initially, Foe mounts her while she tries to conjure up scenes of the island, but cannot. She then claims the right to mount him, since, like the Muse, she "must do whatever lies in her power to father her offspring" (140). She explains the significance of this act to Foe: "The Muse is both goddess and begetter. I was not intended to be the mother of my story, but to beget it. It is not I who am the intended, but you" (126).

FRIDAY'S SILENCE

This "bracing ride" as Foe terms it, is apparently fruitful, for immediately afterwards, he begins to think creatively about the central enigma of Coetzee's tale, Friday. When Barton had first seen Friday casting white petals upon the waves, she rather unimaginatively dismissed the scene as some kind of "superstitious observance" to make the fish run plentifully (31). As we have seen, she later speculated that Friday may have scattered the petals in memory of someone lost in the wreck (87). Foe, now presumably big with book after being tupped by the Muse, surpasses Barton's pale imaginings. Beneath the surface of the waves he envisions *kraken*, legendary sea monsters with "arms as thick as a man's thigh . . . and a beak like an eagle" (140). Friday steers his fragile boat into this menacing realm. Below in the wreckage of the slaveship Foe sees the skeletons of hundreds of Friday's fellow slaves, "the gay little fish . . . flitting through their eyesockets and the hollow cases that had held their hearts" (141). Deadpan Susan at first plays straight-woman to fanciful Foe, saying that she does not believe in monsters and that Friday was not on a boat but a "log of wood" (140), but she soon collaborates in the game. When Foe introduces the metaphor of Friday rowing his log across a great eye in the deep, Barton modifies it to a great "mouth (since we speak in figures). It is for us to open Friday's mouth and hear what it holds: silence, perhaps, or a roar, like the roar of a seashell held to the ear" (142).

Since Friday is mute, Foe suggests that they unlock his thoughts by Susan's teaching him to write. Here Coetzee's linking of Caliban and Friday becomes inescapable:[5] both are the sole slaves of masters of desert isles, both are gatherers of wood, both are called "dull" (Friday by Barton [22], Caliban by Prospero [*The Tempest*, act 1, sc. 2]), and both have language imposed on them, with very different results. Caliban excoriates Prospero, saying,

> You taught me language, and my profit on't
> Is, I know how to curse. The red plague rid you
> For learning me your language!

Coetzee's Friday is less surly and more imaginative. He draws the letters Barton shows him, but like some emerging Dali or Picasso, he chalks on the slate "eyes, open eyes, each set upon a human foot; row upon row of eyes upon feet: walking eyes" (147). Friday's drawing is not only artistically creative but developmentally realistic. A. R. Willcox observes: "In the evolution of art in the history of our species and in the development of the individuals—both European and Bushman—the physioplastic phase precedes the ideoplastic. . . ."[6] Barton, however, considers both her teaching and Friday's learning to be failures. Perhaps she does so because those of us in the West "in following the path of conceptual thought . . . have paid a huge price in the blunting of our perceptions . . . by loss of vividness of visual impressions" (85). Friday has lost his ability to speak, Barton has partially lost her ability to see.

As Barton's narrative draws to a close, she thinks she sees Foe at his desk writing, although it is not Foe, but Friday in Foe's robe and wig, filling his second page with "rows and rows of the letter *o* tightly packed together" (151–52). Barton cries out and moves to snatch the quill from Friday's hand, but Foe admonishes her to let him be, disparaging himself as "an old whore who should ply her trade only in the dark" (151). The third section of the novel ends with Foe advising Barton that tomorrow she should resume her instruction of Friday; she must begin at the beginning: "teach him *a*" (152).

We are left with the substance of three characters: Foe, an aging author who repudiates his earlier aesthetics of the imagination, asking now whether Barton's biological daughter "is substantial or is she a story too?" (152); Susan Barton, negating her former insistence on naturalistic "truth," concluding that her "real" daughter (whom we have never seen), as well as her actress daughter, Foe, and herself "are all alive, we are all substantial, we are all in the same world" (152), presumably of the imagination.

As Foe observes, "You have omitted Friday," who sits drawing and redoubling his enigmatic *o*'s in Foe's cloak and wig. If we look to Daniel Defoe's original Friday, we might find a key to this puzzle. Ur-Friday was an enthusiastic fellow full of speech punctuated with expletive *O*'s: in exultation, "O joy! . . . O glad!" (219); in dejection, "O sorrow! O bad!" (226); in excitement over a bear, "O! O! O!" (287); and in reverence to the creator of all things, the oldest one of all, before the earth and seas, old Benamuckee, who needed no prayers or obeisance because, as Friday said, "All things said O! to him" (213). However, Coetzee's Friday, unlike Defoe's, remains as problematic as the sphinx. One explanation could be that Friday's "*O*" is also a zero, leaving Friday balanced on a pinpoint of time somewhere between the exultation of

Defoe's Friday's "O! O! O!" and Samuel Beckett's favorite quotation
from Democritus, "Nothing is more real than nothing."

THE COLONIAL DILEMMA

Foe does not lend itself as readily as Coetzee's earlier novels to a reading of South African and colonial analogues. Cruso, like the most inflexible of Afrikaners, exhibits an insular insensibility concerning the
outside world. Susan notes that his most remarkable traits are an "indifference to salvation, and habit, and the stubbornness of old age"
(14). However, unlike the economically competitive Afrikaners, Cruso's
industry creates barren terraces; nor are white South Africans likely to
give up their "island" as passively as Cruso did. The apes with "black
faces and black paws" (21), of which Cruso killed so many, are given
only passing notice.

The most viable link to contemporary South Africa in this novel is
obviously the relationship between Susan Barton and sullen, enduring
Friday. Anglo-Franco Barton evidences some racial biases: she finds
Friday's "woodsmoke" (144) smell repulsive, as well as his severed tongue,
"closed behind his lips (as some other mutilations are hidden by cloth-
ing) . . . outwardly he was like any other Negro" (24). Friday's muteness can be read as a symbol of the inexpressible psychic damage absorbed by blacks under racist conditions. The result is a virtually
unbridgeable gap between races and cultures.

This severance of communication is conveyed most poignantly by
Coetzee through the language of music. Two instances stand out. Long
before Barton's advent on the island, Friday had carved a reed flute,
upon which he plays "a tune of six notes, always the same" (26). We
can infer that this is one of the African scales omitting the leading tone,
or seventh degree of the major scale which characterizes Western music.[7] Much annoyed at Friday's playing this "unresolved" (to Western
ears) melody while Cruso is in the throes of a fever, Barton knocks the
flute from Friday's hands, startling him, as she says, "for I had never
lost patience with him before, or indeed paid him much heed" (28).
Later at Foe's house, she finds a set of three recorders and gives Friday
the smallest one to play. To her annoyance, he again plays the same
six-note melody, which first leads her to think of him as a "savage"
flawed by "incuriosity" and "sloth." (95). Reconsidering, she thinks this
may be an opportunity to communicate with Friday through the language of music, and she learns to play his melody on one of the other
recorders. The project is a failure, for though she attempts to play in
unison with him, the music "was not pleasing; there was a subtle dis-
cord all the time" (96). Her attempt to introduce variations leads to a
worse result musically and psychologically, for she suspects that Fri-

day's lack of response is due not to dullness but his "disdain for intercourse" with her. For this slight, real or imagined, Barton has to re-
strain herself from physically striking him.

Toward the end of the novel, when she is frustrated in her attempts
to teach Friday to write English, she tells Foe that she feels like the
fellow in a story who took pity on an old man, carried the man on his
shoulders across a flooding river, and then found that the old man
would not release his good Samaritan, but turned him into a "beast of
burden" (148). This echoes the medical officer's view of Michael K as
an "albatross" about his neck.

Like the officer, Barton's feelings toward her charge fluctuate widely.
Shortly before Cruso's death her impulses seem parental, as she tells
the captain of the *John Hobart*, "inasmuch as Friday is a slave and a
child, it is our duty to care for him in all things, and not abandon him
to a solitude worse than death" (39). A short time later she speaks of
her relation to him as that of a kindly trainer to an animal: "Whenever
I spoke to him I was sure to smile and touch his arm, treating him as
we treat a frightened horse" (41–42). At Foe's house, Barton endeavors
to keep Friday busy and enlarge his vocabulary to prevent idleness from
destroying him. Still, she recognizes, "There are times when benevo-
lence deserts me and I use words only as the shortest way to subject
him to my will. At such times I understand why Cruso preferred not
to disturb his muteness. I understand, that is to say, why a man will
choose to be a slaveholder" (60–61). However, when Barton feels rejected after Friday refuses to become a "consort" with her in a flute or
any other duet, she writes out his freedom papers and attempts to book
safe passage for him back to Africa. Finding none, she picks up her
"burden" again, in her own analogy, like a woman who has borne a
child she does not want, but which she will defend with her life: "Thus
it has become, in a manner of speaking, between Friday and myself. I
do not love him, but he is mine" (111).

Conversely, she once sees Friday whirling and dancing like a dervish
beneath Foe's scarlet robe and associates him with Christ and herself
with doubting Thomas: "What had been hidden from me was revealed
. . . though afterwards I remembered Thomas, who also saw, but could
not be brought to believe till he had put his hand in the wound" (119–
20). Scarcely a moment later, however, she sees him as infinitely malle-
able to the will of others. If she says he is a cannibal, he is a cannibal,
if a laundryman, then a laundryman (121). Her ambivalence reflects
the usual contradictions of those in untenable positions of mastery. In
her last conversation with Foe, Barton succinctly sums up her quan-
dary, as well as South Africa's: "He desires to be liberated, as I do too.
Our desires are plain, his and mine. But how is Friday to recover his
freedom, who has been a slave all his life? That is the true question.

Should I liberate him into a world of wolves and expect to be commended for it?" (148). Thus have colonialists throughout the world expressed their dilemma since the beginning of the end of the colonial era following World War II.

If Coetzee offers no solutions, that is probably because he sees none. One statement of Barton on the problem conjures up the image of Salvador Dali's "Geopoliticus Child Watching the Birth of a New Man," a depiction of a mother and child watching the emergence of a male form from a cracked egg-globe in a rift between the continents of South Africa and South America, from which there trickles a pool of blood. Barton observes of Friday: "He is the child of his silence, a child unborn, a child waiting to be born that cannot be born" (122).

ISLANDS OF THE MIND

The five pages that comprise the concluding fourth selection of *Foe* are a protean dreamlike evocation of the realm of the dead, a revisitation both on land and beneath the sea to the two major settings of this novel three hundred years afterwards (157). The narrator is no longer Susan Barton, but an interloper who knows the text of *Foe* and who drifts among the shades that were the characters, perhaps the consciousness that breathed life into them to begin with.

The first scene occurs at the house of Foe. The "daughter" is lying on a stair landing, wrapped in an "endless" scarf. "She weighs no more than a sack of straw" (153). Inside are the figures of a man and a woman in bed—we infer they are Foe and Susan—their taut skin "dry as paper." They lie side by side, not touching; their faces are skull-like, smiling. Friday lies on the floor amid old dust. He is breathing, there is a faint pulse. The visitor puts an ear to Friday's mouth and can hear "the faintest faraway roar: as she [Barton, (142)] said, the roar of the waves in a seashell; and over that, as if once or twice a violin-string were touched, the whine of the wind and the cry of a bird" (154).

As is the case with several scenes in *In the Heart of the Country*, the preceding is recapitulated, with slight variations, suggesting that there are multiple versions of reality. The visitor enters again, finds the couple in bed, this time with the woman's head nestled in the man's arm. He notes that Friday has a scar about his neck, as from a rope or chain. Coetzee then employs a device that Nabokov and others have used, a kind of cinematic "dissolve" that transports a character wherever consciousness takes him or her. The visitor finds on a table the top leaf of a yellowed manuscript bearing the opening words of Barton's narrative. "At last I could row no further." As she did, he "slips overboard," but instead of finding the island, drifts "south toward the realm of the whales and eternal ice" (155) amid the white petals cast by Friday, then dives into the deep. Coetzee had foreshadowed this submersion earlier when Susan told Foe, "If Friday cannot tell us what he sees, is Friday in my story any more than a figuring (or prefiguring) of another diver?" (142).

The images Coetzee employs here are darkly dreamlike. The diver finds the wreck of a huge ship, its timbers black, in its hull, an oozing mudlike quicksand. "There are no swarms of gay little fish" (156) as Foe fancied. In the cabin the water is "still and dead," as it was yesterday, as it was three hundred years ago. Inside there is an eerie scene, held constant for centuries. Susan Barton and her dead captain-lover "float like stars," "fat as pigs in their white nightclothes, their limbs extending stiffly from their trunks, their hands, puckered from long immersion, held out in blessing" (157).

Finally, the diver finds Friday, half covered with sand, who does not answer the questions asked of him, for it is not a place of words: "This is a place where bodies are their own signs. It is the home of Friday" (157). The diver lies beside Friday, face to face, and from Friday's mouth issues a "slow stream, without breath . . . it runs northward and southward to the ends of the earth. Soft and cold, dark and unending, it beats against my eyelids, against the skin of my face" (157).

In this enigmatic ending, so gracefully written, the themes of narrative art and colonialism coalesce. At one point Barton asked herself, if Friday "was not a slave, was he nevertheless not the helpless captive of my desire to have our story told?" (150). Foe offers another explanation: "it is possible that some of us are not written, but merely are; or else (I think principally of Friday) are written by another and darker author" (143). Francis King gave a similar reading in a review, seeing Friday as one of those characters who "represent that bedrock of the individual personality to which no novelist, however piercing his intuition, can ever hope to tunnel deep enough to reach."[8]

In terms of both the narrative and colonial themes, it is significant that Friday is submerged, unresolved, and that of all the characters, he is the only one still apparently alive. The "slow stream" emerging from Friday' mouth and running "to the ends of the earth . . . dark and unending" (157), may well foreshadow the impending outrage of all of the silent ones waiting to break their bonds.

STORYTELLING

There are clearly powerful elements in *Foe*, but whether or not the novel coalesces into a powerful artistic whole is another question. Coetzee's prose style is as graceful and incisive as ever, as most of the preceding quotations evidence and reviewers confirm: Gardam notes that the prose "is nearer to poetry than narrative";[9] Donoghue speaks of

the "radiance" of the style;[10] Koenig praises the "needle-sharp preci-
sion of Coetzee's mock-eighteenth-century prose";[11] and King extols
"the beauty of the style—measured, limpid, euphonious" ("Telling Stories," 33).

Moreover, Susan Barton is one of Coetzee's most memorable and
vibrant characters, clearly overshadowing the three principal male figures, Cruso, Foe, and Friday. However, while the interactions between
imaginative, energetic Susan and stolid Cruso are engaging, they end
with his death one-third of the way into the novel; her aesthetic exchanges with pragmatic Foe are thought-provoking, but do not begin
until the last third of the novel; and silent Friday does not communicate with Barton at all, remaining throughout more a symbol than a
character. As Nina Auerbach observes from a feminist perspective, the
three men "merge into one ungiving male who will not share his being
with her."[12]

The idea of placing Barton, Cruso, and Friday on the island is inge-
nious, if not brilliant. The interaction between Barton's energetic prac-
ticality and Cruso's and Friday's preoccupation with building their Absurdist terraces and walls could seemingly have been sustained, in the
fashion of Beckett, indefinitely. It may be that Coetzee curtailed the
project because the Beckettian overtones became too evident. Whatever
the reason, one wishes that he had devised something more engaging
for Barton to do after leaving the island than what she does.

The problem with the two London sections, which comprise two-thirds
of the novel, is that too little happens. In the first section, Barton is
sequestered in Foe's Clock Lane house with mute Friday, whom she
periodically attempts to teach words, manners, and gardening. Much
of the rest of her time is spent thinking about the nature of narrative,
either by herself or in her correspondence to Foe, which he may or
may not have answered (Barton mentions Foe's responses, but we are
not shown his letters). The epistolary mode is by nature reflective, not
active, as Barton repeatedly reminds us:

> "The days pass on and no word from you" (61).
> "How much of my life consists in waiting" (66).
> "I talk to Friday as old women talk to cats, out of loneliness" (77).
> "Days pass. Nothing changes" (87).

The result is that there is a rather long section of the novel in which
stasis seems to be the controlling element.

Another factor contributing to the lack of event in *Foe* is Coetzee's
concern, voiced through Barton and Foe, with theories of narrative art.
In an interview on 28 August 1985, when Coetzee was probably still
working on *Foe* (published fall, 1986), he stated, "I believe very strongly

in the critical activity of the literary critic—and I hope that I bring across my fiction writing some of that same concern with the importance of criticism, which is to me a matter of taking nothing for granted."[13] When this means presenting theory within a novel, the premise has more appeal to the writer than to most readers. Kendrick notes that Coetzee's concern with theory weakens *Foe* because "the dilemma it posits belongs to him, not his characters."[14] Auerbach observes that "although *Foe* is a brilliant disquisition on the making of fictions . . . it never quite comes to life. Uncharacteristically, Coetzee speaks here as a writer writing for other writers, rather than as an appalled representative of humanity" ("Novel," 37). Donoghue notes that Foe "has evidently been reading Jacques Derrida's 'De la Grammatologie' " ("Her Man Friday," 27), given Foe's observations on the divergent significations of words in speech and writing. The essence of these criticisms is that, in a work of fiction, theories about fiction are best suggested implicitly, rather than stated through direct discourse.

In a brief, thoughtful, and informed essay, George Packer sums up the successes and failures of *Foe*, placing this fifth novel within the context of Coetzee's other works. He notes that *Foe* continues the theme of oppression that pervades all of Coetzee's works, and that the agency of oppression here is language, which also plays an important part in *In the Heart of the Country*. In Packer's reading, there is a dichotomy:

On one side are the island, Cruso and Friday, the hidden truth, and the muteness which goes along with victimization; on the other side, London, Foe, illusion, and speech which is linked to power. Susan tries to mediate between these, to bring Friday to Foe and silence to speech; but there is no mediation.[15]

Packer contends that *Foe* presents "a brilliant debate about speech and writing, truth and illusion"; that it generally "avoids the excessive cleverness of the self-regarding novel," yet it does not reach the intensity of Coetzee's best work, in which the "straightforward story . . . seems too urgent to be diverted" (404). Packer concludes that "*Foe* reads as if Coetzee started out to reinvent Defoe's famous tale through a woman's eyes, became intrigued with the linguistic and philosophical implications, and ended up writing a commentary on the elusiveness of his own project" (404). This may be assuming too much, but on the basis of the text, it seems a reasonable surmise.

Finally, remarks that Coetzee made in two interviews are germane. Asked if *Foe* could be seen as "something of a retreat from the South African situation," he replied in February 1987, "*Foe* is a retreat from the South African situation in a narrow temporal perspective. It is not a retreat from the subject of colonialism or from questions of power. What you call 'the nature and processes of fiction' may also be called the question of *who writes*? Who takes up the position of power, pen in hand?" (Morphet interview, 462).

Asked if he regarded himself as a "metaphysical novelist" who also gives the reader "all the enjoyment of reading a novel," he replied in August 1985: "All attempts to eradicate storytelling from the novel are doomed . . . and here I think particularly of the Nouveau Roman. . . . I would regard these as philosophical experiments, immensely important for philosophical experiment with the nature of fiction, but experiments from which we finally have to retreat . . . if we are ever going back to the novel, go back to story-telling" (Sévry interview, 6).

Coetzee's observations speak well enough for themselves.

NOTES

My review article based on this chapter is "J. M. Coetzee's *Foe*: The Muse, the Absurd, and the Colonial Dilemma," *World Literature Written in English* 27, no. 2 (Autumn 1987): 207–15.

1. Michiko Kakutani, *"Foe*, by J. M. Coetzee," *New York Times*, 11 February 1987, 19.

2. Daniel Defoe, *Robinson Crusoe* (New York: New American Library, 1961), 202; all references are to this edition.

3. Teresa Dovey, *The Novels of J. M. Coetzee: Lacanian Allegories*, Human Sciences Research Council Publication Series, no. 86 (Johannesburg: Ad. Donker, 1988), 342.

4. See Henry Fielding, *Joseph Andrews*, author's preface; and *Tom Jones*, the first chapters of bks. 2, 5, and 9.

5. I am indebted to my colleague Norman Sanders for suggesting the link between Caliban and Friday.

6. A. R. Wilcox, *Rock Paintings of the Drakensberg* (London: Max Parrish, 1956), 81.

7. Thanks to my colleague Steve Young for information concerning African music.

8. Francis King, "Telling Stories, Telling Tales, Telling Fiction," *Spectator* 257–8254 (20 September 1986): 33.

9. Jane Gardam, "The Only Story," *Sunday Times Review*, (7 September 1986): 49.

10. Dennis Donoghue, "Her Man Friday," *New York Times Book Review*, 22 February 1987, 26.

11. Rhoda Koenig, "Taking Liberties," *New York* 20 (9 February 1987): 91.

12. Nina Auerbach, "A Novel of Her Own," *New Republic* 3764 (9 March 1987): 37.

13. J. M. Coetzee in interview with Jean Sévry, *Commonwealth* 9, no. 1 (Autumn 1986): 6.

14. Walter Kendrick, *"Foe," Boston Review* 12, no. 1 (February 1987): 26.

15. George Packer, "Blind Alleys," *Nation* 244 (28 March 1987): 404.

8

End Game: The Great South African Novel and the Cockroach

After receiving the Booker-McConnell Prize for *Life and Times of Michael K*, Coetzee published an essay in 1983 entitled "The Great South African Novel."[1] In this he speaks of the "remarkably respectful hearing" which the world gives to South African writers, a consequence, he believes, of the world's concern with the relationship of the "*coloniser* to the *colonised*," the dominion of "white" people over other peoples, which in most other parts of the world has diminished in varying degrees in the last half-century. The world looks for truth less from journalists than from artists, he says, because of a traditional belief in the West that "the artist, answerable to no man, only to his own art and conscience, is the nearest thing to a truth-teller we are likely to have," a belief which, Coetzee suggests, may or may not be valid, but which nevertheless prevails (74).

Coetzee's purpose in this essay is twofold: to define the necessary elements of any Great National Novel, and to determine whether anyone is ever likely to write a Great South African Novel. He contends that any such work must meet at least three criteria; it must

1. contain characterizations of society at all levels during the time in which it is set
2. employ realistic techniques that make the work accessible to most of the reading public
3. make the local universal

Three works which he feels qualify as Great National Novels are *Tom Jones*, *Anna Karenina*, and *Moby Dick*; three which do not, despite their literary merit, are *Clarissa*, *The Idiot*, and *The Golden Bowl*. García Már-

quez's *One Hundred Years of Solitude* qualifies, and also demonstrates that
the idea of a Great National Novel is not a thing of the past (77).

Coetzee observes that the world is eager for a major black writer
from South Africa to "tell them what it is *really* like," although "This
writer has not yet come" (74). He believes that Nadine Gordimer and
André Brink are South African writers likely to create a Great Novel,
but that the whole idea of a Great South African Novel is problematical. There are several reasons for this, the principal one being that
South Africa does not constitute a national or ethnic unity, but rather,
is a society "marked by disunity, fragmentation, internal antagonisms,
anomie, and above all by a multiplicity of languages" (79): The "native
(*inheems*) South African languages," as well as Afrikaans, have little cur-
rency outside the country. On the other hand, English, the dominant
language in world literature and Coetzee's chosen medium, has not established a "South African linguistic consciousness" even after two
hundred years (79).

Coetzee concludes that if anyone ever writes a Great South African
Novel, as he has defined it, he is not likely to be the author. I submit
that some of Coetzee's writing is already arguably great: *In the Heart of
the Country*, *Waiting for the Barbarians*, and *Life and Times of Michael K.*
Each of these conveys a precise understanding and skillful use of language, as well as a tactile sense of place. Each convincingly portrays the
psychological reality of the characters, along with an understanding of
the complexity of ethical decisions made in real life; there is also a
sense of the unyielding movement of the forces of history—especially
of colonialism. All of these novels succeed in transforming their stories
into what Brink calls "the universality of allegory,"[2] something on the
border of myth-making.

This mythic quality is closely related to another aspect of Coetzee's
fiction, which Stephen Watson describes:

In Coetzee's transfiguring myths, in his penchant for situations way beyond the
bounds of society, in the very asceticism of his style which gave no place to any
"naturalistic arbitrariness," there seemed to lurk a quasi-religious impulse which,
whether recognized by the reader or not, only made his work that much more
compelling.[3]

This sense of what I will call sanctity of life, is pervasive. It is in Magda's "closing plangencies" as she acknowledges that she is "corrupted
to the bone with the beauty of this forsaken world" (139). It is present
in her solitary appeals to the sky-gods, to her dead father—to anyone—
for understanding. It is found in the thought-tormented magistrate's
ritual oiling of the barbarian girl's feet, in his brave refusal to cooperate
with the torturers, and in his suffering when they torture him. It is

present in Michael K's gentle nurturing of the earth, in his reverence for the earth's bounty, and in his awareness that someone must keep "the idea of gardening" alive.

By his own definition, Coetzee has not written the Great South African Novel. It matters little. What is important is that he, as an artist and a human being, is a "truth-teller." I quote again Coetzee's observation on the experience of being a novelist living in South Africa:

For the writer the deeper problem is *not* to allow himself to be impaled on the dilemma proposed by the state, namely, either to ignore its obscenities or else to produce representations of them. The true challenge is how not to play the game by the rules of the state, how to establish one's own authority.[4]

However, to be a "truth-teller," a storyteller on one's own terms, an author must resist ideological pressures from quarters other than the state.

THE COCKROACH

At a book-fest in Cape Town late in 1987, Coetzee gave a speech which was reprinted in a local literary journal, *Upstream*.[5] His topic is the status of the novel in South Africa in the 1980s, specifically, the tendency of contemporary events, "history," and "ideological pressure" to "subsume the novel," to reduce fiction to a supplement to history (2). The novel, Coetzee argues, "cannot be both autonomous and supplementary" (3). He then makes an important distinction: the autonomous novel "evolves its own paradigms and myths . . . perhaps going so far as to show up the mythic status of history—in other words, demythologizing history" (3). While Coetzee does not make reference to his own works in this speech, his definition of the autonomous novel clearly applies, as we have seen, to *Dusklands, In the Heart of the Country, Waiting for the Barbarians, Life and Times of Michael K*, and to a lesser extent, *Foe*.

Midway in his address, Coetzee speaks as one embattled, under attack, as indeed he has been, by those who fault what they perceive as the absence, or at best the parabolic nature, of political engagement in his fiction. In response to such attacks, he draws an analogy from a constant theme in his novels: "in South Africa the colonization of the novel by the discourse of history is proceeding with alarming rapidity. I speak, therefore—to use a figure—as a member of a tribe threatened with colonization" (3). He observes that history will "try to claim primacy, claim to be a master-form of discourse," although history is simply a discourse different in kind from the discourse of the novel. "The categories of history are not privileged," Coetzee argues, "They do not reside in reality, they are a certain construction put upon reality" (4).

What then may we expect of the future of the "autonomous novel," of storytelling that is not ancillary to history, given the current explosive social and political pressures in South Africa, and elsewhere, for that matter? In an incisive parable, Coetzee argues that the art of the story form will endure:

Storytelling is another, an other mode of thinking. It is more venerable than history, as ancient as the cockroach. . . . Like cockroaches, stories can be consumed. All you need to do is tear off the wings and sprinkle a little salt on them. . . . Cockroaches can also be colonized. You can capture them in a cockroach trap, breed them (quite easily), herd them together in cockroach farms. . . . You can do minute dissections of their respiratory systems. . . . You can, if you wish, dry them and powder them and mix them with high explosives and make bombs of them. You can even make up stories about them, as Kafka did, although this is quite hard. One of the things you cannot—apparently—do is eradicate them. They breed, as the figure has it, like flies, and under the harshest circumstances. . . . It is said that they will still be around when we and all our artifacts have disappeared. (4)

Coetzee concludes his "cockroach speech" by observing that the meanings of parables are hard to pin down. Thus, parables are a mode of storytelling favored by "marginal groups," those who are not part of the main current of history (4). The meaning of Coetzee's parable should be clear enough by now to the audience of this book. Stories survive the rules of ideological censorship, as Coetzee says in his speech, through

their faculty of making and changing their own rules. There is a game going on between the covers of the book, but it is not always the game you think it is. No matter what it may appear to be doing, the story may not really be playing the game you call Class Conflict or the game called Male Domination or any of the other games in the games handbook. (3–4)

Put another way, the story quite simply may be playing the game of being a story, as elusive and enduring as the cockroach, scuttling within the walls of history. I close by quoting one of the epigraphs which opens this book, a statement which Coetzee made to a group of novice writers in a workshop in 1984:

Whereas in the kind of game I am talking about
you can change the rules if you are good enough.
You can change the rules for everybody if you are good enough,
You can change the game.

NOTES

1. J. M. Coetzee, "The Great South African Novel," *Leadership SA 2* (Summer 1983): 74–79.

2. André Brink, "Writing Against Big Brother: Notes on Apocalyptic Fiction in South Africa," *World Literature Today*, 58, no. 2 (1984): 192.

3. Stephen Watson, "Colonialism in the Novels of J. M. Coetzee," *Research in African Literatures* 17 (1986): 372.

4. J. M. Coetzee, "Into the Dark Chamber: The Novelist and South Africa," *New York Times Book Review*, 22 January 1986, 13.

5. J. M. Coetzee, "The Novel Today," *Upstream* 6, no. 1 (Summer 1988): 2–5. I am indebted to Stephen Watson for sending me the offprint from this journal, which is not readily available in the United States. The article states that Coetzee's speech was given at the "1987 Weekly Mail Book Week in Cape Town," and Coetzee mentions that he is speaking in the "Baxter Theatre." (3)

Bibliography

Abrahams, Lionel. "Reflections in a Mirror." *Snarl* 1, no. 1 (1974): 2–3.

Alter, Robert. *Partial Magic: The Novel as a Self-conscious Genre.* Berkeley: Univ. of California Press, 1975.

Auerbach, Nina. "A Novel of Her Own." Review of *Foe* by J. M. Coetzee. *New Republic* 3764 (9 March 1987): 36–38.

Bakewell, Charles. *Source Book in Ancient Philosophy.* New York: Gordian, 1973.

Barnett, Ursla A. *A Vision of Order: A Study of Black South African Literature in English.* London: S. Browne, 1983.

Barrow, Brian. *South African People.* Cape Town: Macdonald, 1977.

Beardsley, Monroe C. "Dostoevsky's Metaphor of the Underground." *Journal of the History of Ideas* 3 (June 1942): 265–90.

Beckett, Samuel. *First Love and Other Stories.* New York: Grove, 1974.

Bernard, Ian. "Coetzee, J. M." In *Postmodern Fiction: A Bio-Bibliographical Guide,* edited by Larry McCaffery, 305–8. New York: Greenwood Press, 1986.

Boyd, Michael. *The Reflexive Novel: Fiction as Critique.* Lewisburg: Bucknell Univ. Press, 1983.

Brewer, John D. *After Soweto.* New York: Clarendon, 1986.

Brink, André. "Writing Against Big Brother: Notes on Apocalyptic Fiction in South Africa." *World Literature Today* 58, no.2 (1984): 189–94.

Bunn, David, and Jane Taylor, eds. *From South Africa.* Special issue of *Tri-Quarterly.* Evanston: Northwestern Univ. Press, 1987.

Burgess, Anthony. "The Beast Within." Review of *Waiting for the Barbarians* by J. M. Coetzee. *New York* 15 (26 April 1982): 88–90.

Camus, Albert. *The Plague.* New York: Random House, 1948.

Castillo, Debra A. "The Composition of the Self in Coetzee's *Waiting for the Barbarians.*" *Critique* 27, no. 2 (Winter 1986): 78–90.

Cavafy, Constantin (also Kavafis or Kabaphes). *Collected Poems.* Translated by Edmund Keeley and Philip Sherrard; edited by George Savidis. Princeton: Princeton Univ. Press, 1975.

Christie, Sarah, Geoffrey Hutchings, and Don Maclennan. *Perspectives on South African Fiction.* Johannesburg: Ad. Donker, 1980.

"Coetzee, Getting Prize, Denounces Apartheid." *New York Times,* 11 April 1987, 14.

Coetzee, J[ohn] M[axwell]. "Achterberg's 'Ballade van de gasfitter': The Mystery of I and You." *PMLA* 92 (1977): 285–96.

———. "The Agentless Sentence as Rhetorical Device." *Language and Style: An International Journal* 13, no. 1 (1980): 26–34.

———. "Alex La Guma and the Responsibilities of the South African Writer." *Journal of the New African Literature and the Arts* 9/10 (1971): 5–11.

———. "Anthropology and the Hottentots." *Semiotica* 54 (1985): 87–95.

———. "Apartheid: La littérature mutilée" (translation of Coetzee's Jerusalem Prize acceptance speech). *Le Nouvel Observateur* 1174 (8–14 May 1987): 57–58.

———. "Art and Apartheid." *New Republic* 3612 (9 April 1984): 25–28.

———. Audiotape. Interview with Dick Penner. Lexington, Ky. 6 March 1984.

———. Audiotape. Introduction to readings from *In the Heart of the Country, Waiting for the Barbarians,* and *Life and Times of Michael K.* Lexington, Ky. 5 March 1984.

———. Audiotape. Lecture on Dostoevsky. Lexington, Ky. 5 March 1984.

———. Audiotape. Remarks during writers' workshop. Lexington, Ky. 6 March 1984.

———. "Blood, Flaw, Taint, Degeneration: The Case of Sarah Gertrude Millin." *English Studies in Africa: A Journal of the Humanities* 23 (1980): 41–58.

———. "Captain America in American Mythology." *University of Cape Town Studies in English* 6 (1976): 33–39.

———. "The Comedy of Point of View in Beckett's *Murphy.*" *Critique: Studies in Modern Fiction* 12, no. 2 (1970): 19–27.

———. "Confession and Double Thoughts: Tolstoy, Rousseau, Dostoevsky." *Comparative Literature* 37, no. 3 (Summer 1985): 193–232.

———. *Dusklands.* Johannesburg: Raven Press, 1974. London: Secker and Warburg, 1982. New York: Viking Penguin, 1985.

———. "The English Fiction of Samuel Beckett: An Essay in Stylistic Analysis." Ph.D. Diss., University of Texas, 1969.

———. "Farm Novel and *Plaasroman* in South Africa." *English in Africa* 13, no. 2 (October 1986): 1–19.

———. "The First Sentence of Yvonne Burgess's *The Strike.*" *English in Africa* 3, no. 1 (1976): 47–48.

———. *Foe.* London: Secker and Warburg, 1986. New York: Viking Penguin, 1987.

———. "The Great South African Novel." *Leadership SA 2* (Summer 1983): 74–79.

———. "How I Learned About America—and Africa—in Texas." *New York Times Book Review,* 9 April 1984, 9.

———. "Idleness in South Africa." *Social Dynamics* 8 (1982): 1–13.

———. *In the Heart of the Country.* London: Secker and Warburg, 1977. Published under the title *From the Heart of the Country.* New York: Harper and Row, 1977. Johannesburg: Raven, 1978 [bilingual edition]. New York: Viking Penguin, 1982.

———. Interview with Jean Sévry. *Commonwealth* 9, no. 1 (Autumn 1986): 1–7.

———. Interview with Folke Rhedin. *Kunapipi* 6, no. 1 (1984): 6–11.

———. Interview with Stephen Watson. *Speak* 1, no. 3 (1978): 21–24.

———. Interview with Tony Morphet. *From South Africa*. Special issue of *Tri-Quarterly*. Evanston: Northwestern Univ. Press, 1987: 454–64.

———. Interview with Avril Herber. *Conversations*. Johannesburg: Bateleur, 1979: 174–78.

———. "Into the Dark Chamber: The Novelist and South Africa." *New York Times Book Review*, 12 January 1986, 13, 35, 53.

———. "Introduction." Marcellus Emants, *Posthumous Confession*. Translated by J. M. Coetzee. London: Quartet Books, 1987. Boston: Twayne, 1975.

———. *A Land Apart: A South African Reader*. Edited by J. M. Coetzee and André Brink. London and Boston: Faber and Faber, 1986.

———. *Life and Times of Michael K*. London: Secker and Warburg, 1983. New York: Viking Penguin, 1984.

———. "Lineal Consciousness in the Farm Novels of C. M. van den Heever." *Tijdschrift voor Nederlands en Afrikaans*. Cologne: September 1985: 49–74.

———. "Linguistics and Literature." In *An Introduction to Contemporary Literary Theory*, edited by Rory Ryan and Susan van Zyl, 41–52. Johannesburg: Ad. Donker, 1982.

———. "Listening to Afrikaners." *New York Times Book Review*, 14 April 1985, 3, 28.

———. "Man's Fate in the Novels of Alex La Guma." *Studies in Black Literature* 5, no. 1 (1974): 16–23.

———. "The Manuscript Revisions of Beckett's *Watt*." *Journal of Modern Literature* 2 (1972): 472–80.

———. Nabokov's *Pale Fire* and the Primacy of Art." *University of Cape Town Studies in English* 5 (1974): 1–7.

———. "Newton and the Ideal of a Transparent Scientific Language." *Journal of Literary Semantics* 11, no. 2 (October 1982): 3–13.

———. "A Note of Writing." In *Momentum: On Recent South African Writing*, edited by M. J. Daymond, J. U. Jacobs, and M. Lenta, 11–13. Pietermaritzburg, South Africa: Natal Univ. Press, 1984.

———. "The Novel Today." *Upstream* 6, no. 1 (Summer 1988): 2–5.

———. "On the Edge of Revelation." *New York Review* 18 (December 1986): 10, 12.

———. "Out of Africa!" *American Film* (March 1987): 19–23.

———. "Pauline Smith and the Afrikaans Language." *English in Africa* 8, no. 1 (1981): 25–32.

———. "A Prisoner of the Thought Police." *New York Times Book Review*, 31 May 1987, 9, 46.

———. "The Rhetoric of the Passive in English." *Linguistics: An Interdisciplinary Journal of the Language Sciences* 18 (1980): 199–221.

———. "Samuel Beckett's Lessness: An Exercise in Decomposition." *Computers and the Humanities* 7 (1973): 195–98.

———. "Samuel Beckett and the Temptations of Style." *Theoria* 41 (1973): 45–50.

———. "Satyagraha in Durban." *New York Review of Books* 32, no. 16 (24 October 1985): 12–13.

———. "Statistical Indices of 'Difficulty.' " *Language & Style* 2 (1969): 226–32.

———. "Surreal Metaphors and Random Proceses." *Journal of Literary Semantics* 8 (1979): 22–30.

———. "Tales of Afrikaners." *New York Times Magazine* 135 (9 March 1986): 19, 21–2, 74–75.

———. "Tales Out of School." *New Republic* 3753 (22 December 1986): 36–38.

———. "The Taming of D. H. Lawrence." *New York Review of Books* 37, no. 21 & 22 (16 January 1986): 33–35.

———. "Time, Tense and Aspect in Kafka's 'The Burrow.' " *MLN* 96, no. 3 (April 1981): 556–79.

———. "Triangular Structures of Desire in Advertising." *Critical Arts* 1 (1980): 34–41.

———. "Truth in Autobiography." Inaugural lecture, Univ. of Capetown, New Series 94 (3 October 1984): 1–6.

———. "Waiting for Mandela." *New York Review of Books* 33, no. 8 (8 May 1986): 3, 6, 8.

———. *Waiting for the Barbarians*. London: Secker and Warburg, 1980. New York: Viking Penguin, 1982.

———. *White Writing: On the Culture of Letters in South Africa*. New Haven and London: Yale Univ. Press, 1988.

———. "The White Man's Burden." *Speak* (Cape Town) 1 (1977): 4–7.

———. "The White Tribe." *Vogue* (March 1986): 490-91, 543-44.

"Coetzee, J[ohn] M." *Current Biography* 48, no. 1 (January 1987): 18–21.

Crapanzano, Vincent. *Waiting: The Whites in South Africa*. New York: Random House, 1985.

Crew, Jonathan. *"Dusklands." Contrast* 9, no. 11 (1974): 90–95.

Darras, Jacques. "Apartheid Coté Blanc." [On *In the Heart of the Country*] *Esprit* (Paris) 2 (1983): 15–25.

Davenport, T. R. H. *South Africa: A Modern History*. London: Macmillan, 1985.

Daymond, M. J., et al., eds. *Momentum: On Recent South African Writing*. Pietermaritzburg, South Africa: Univ. of Natal Press, 1984.

Defoe, Daniel. *Robinson Crusoe*. New York: New American Library, 1961.

Dodd, Josephine. "Naming and Framing: Naturalization and Colonization in J. M. Coetzee's *In the Heart of the Country*." *World Literature Written in English* 27, no. 2 (Autumn 1987): 153–61.

Donoghue, Dennis. "Her Man Friday." Review of *Foe* by J. M. Coetzee. *New York Times Book Review*, 22 February 1987, 1, 26–27.

Dostoevsky, Fyodor, *Notes from Underground*. Translated with introduction by Ralph Matlaw. New York: Dutton, 1960.

Dovey, Teresa. *The Novels of J. M. Coetzee: Lacanian Allegories*. Human Sciences Research Council Publication Series, no. 86. Johannesburg: Ad. Donker, 1988. (Revision of Dovey's Ph.D. diss. "The Lacanian Subject in the Novels of J. M. Coetzee," Univ. Melbourne, 1986.)

Du Plessis, Menan. "Towards a New Materialism." *Contrast* 13, no. 4 (1983): 77–87.

Encyclopedia of Southern Africa. 5th ed. London: Frederick Warne & Co. 1970.

Enright, D. J. "Visions and Revisions." Review of *Foe* by J. M. Coetzee. *New York Review of Books* 34, no. 9 (28 May 1987): 18–20.

———. "The Thing Itself." Review of *Life and Times of Michael K* by J. M. Coetzee. *Times Literary Supplement* (London: 30 September 1983): 1035.

Fielding, Henry. *The History of the Adventures of Joseph Andrews.* New York: Modern Library, 1950.

———. *The History of Tom Jones.* New York: Random House, 1950.

Flower, Dean. "Fiction Chronicle." Review of *Life and Times of Michael K* by J. M. Coetzee. *Hudson Review* 37, no. 2 (Summer 1984): 312–15.

Furbank, P. N. "Mistress, Muse, and Begetter." Review of *Foe* by J. M. Coetzee. *Times Literary Supplement* 4354 (12 September 1986): 995.

Gakwandi, Shatto A. *The Novel and Contemporary Experience in South Africa.* London: Heinemann, 1977.

Gardam, Jane. "The Only Story." Review of *Foe* by J. M. Coetzee. *Sunday Times Review* (7 September 1986): 49.

Gardiner, Allan. "J. M. Coetzee's *Dusklands*: Colonial Encounters of the Robinsonian Kind." *World Literature Written in English* 27, no. 2 (Autumn 1987): 174–84.

Gilbert, Harriet. "Island Stories." Review of *Foe* by J. M. Coetzee. *New Statesman* 112: 2894 (12 September 1986): 29.

Gillmer, Joan. "The Motif of the Damaged Child in the Work of J. M. Coetzee." In *Momentum: On Recent South African Writing.* edited by M. J. Daymond et al., 107–20. Pietermaritzburg, South Africa: Univ. of Natal Press, 1984.

Glendinning, Victoria. "A Harsh Voice Crying in the Wilderness." Review of *Dusklands* by J. M. Coetzee. *Sunday Times* (London), 23 January 1983, 45.

Gordimer, Nadine. "The Idea of Gardening." Review of *Life and Times of Michael K,* by J. M. Coetzee. *New York Review of Books,* 2 February 1984, 3, 6.

Gorman, G. E. *The South African Novel in English Since 1950.* Boston: G. K. Hall, 1978.

Gray, Rosemary. "J. M. Coetzee's *Dusklands*: Of War and War's Alarms." *Commonwealth* 9, no. 1 (Autumn 1986): 32–43.

Gray, Stephen. *Southern African Literature: An Introduction.* New York: Harper, 1979.

Greene, Graham. *The Power and the Glory.* New York: Bantam, 1968.

Griffin, Robert J., and William A. Freedman. "Machines and Animals: Pervasive Motifs in *The Grapes of Wrath.*" In *John Steinbeck, The Grapes of Wrath, Text and Criticism.* Edited by Peter Lisca, 769–83. New York: Penguin, 1977.

Groot Woordeboek: Afrikaans-Engles. 12th ed. Edited by Matthy Kritzinger. Pretoria: J. L. van Schaik, 1981.

Haluska, Jan. "Master and Salve in the First Four Novels of J. M. Coetzee." Ph.D. diss., University of Tennessee, 1987.

Harvey, C. J. D. Review of *Waiting for the Barbarians* by J. M. Coetzee. *Standpunte* 34 (August 1981): 3–8.

Haywood, Christopher. *Aspects of South African Literature.* New York: Africana, 1976.

Hegel, Georg Wilhelm Friedrich. *Reason in History.* New York: Liberal Arts Press, 1953.

Henry, Charles. "Notes on Magda." unpublished paper.

Heraclitus. *The Cosmic Fragments.* Edited by G. S. Kirk. Cambridge: Cambridge Univ. Press, 1954.

————. *Heraclitus of Ephesus.* Edited by Geoffrey Stephen. Cambridge: Cambridge Univ. Press, 1954.

Howe, Irving. "Waiting for the Barbarians." Review of *Waiting for the Barbarians* by J. M. Coetzee. *New York Times Book Review* 87 (18 April 1982): 1, 36.

Hutcheon, Linda. *Narcissistic Narrative: The Metafictional Paradox.* Waterloo, Ont.: Wilfrid Laurier Univ. Press, 1980.

"J(ohn) M. Coetzee." *Contemporary Literary Criticism,* vol. 33, edited by Daniel G. Marowski and Jean C. Stine. Detroit: Gale Research, 1985.

Kafka, Franz. "A Hunger Artist." *The Penal Colony.* Translated by Willa and Edwin Muir. New York: Schocken Books, 1961.

Kakutani, Michiko. "Foe, By J. M. Coetzee." *New York Times,* 11 February 1987, 19.

Kendrick, Walter. "*Foe.*" Review of *Foe* by J. M. Coetzee. *Boston Review* 12, no. 1 (February 1987): 26.

King, Bruce Alvin. *The New English Literatures.* London: Macmillan, 1980.

King, Francis. "Telling Stories, Telling Tales, Telling Fiction." Review of *Foe* by J. M. Coetzee. *Spectator* 257–8254 (20 September 1986): 33.

Knox-Shaw, Peter. "*Dusklands*: A Metaphysics of Violence." *Commonwealth Novel in English* 14, no. 1 (1983): 65–81.

Koenig, Rhoda. "Taking Liberties." Review of *Foe* by J. M. Coetzee. *New York* 20 (9 February 1987): 91–92.

Kramer, Jane. "In the Garrison." Review of *Waiting for the Barbarians* by J. M. Coetzee. *New York Times* 29 (2 December 1982): 8–12.

Lao-Tsu. *Tao Te Ching.* Translated by Gia-Fu Feng and Jane English. New York: Random House, 1972.

Lewis, Peter. "Types of Tyranny." Review of *Waiting for the Barbarians* by J. M. Coetzee. *Times Literary Supplement* 7 (November 1980): 1270.

"Lifting Coetzee's Veil." *World Press Review* 32, no. 7 (July 1985): 60.

McDaniel, Ellen. "Quiet Heroism in *Life and Times of Michael K.*" *Notes on Contemporary Literature* 15, no. 1 (January 1985): 11–12.

McEwan, Neil. *Africa and the Novel.* London and Basingstoke: Macmillan, 1983.

Maes-Jelinek, Hena. "Ambivalent Clio: J. M. Coetzee's *In the Heart of the Country* and Wilson Harris's *Carnival.*" *Journal of Commonwealth Literature* 22, no. 1 (1987): 87–98.

Magubane, Peter. *Magubane's South Africa.* New York: Knopf, 1978.

Mandela, Nelson. *No Easy Walk to Freedom.* New York: Basic Books, 1965.

Martin, Richard G. "Narrative, History, Ideology: A Study of *Waiting for the Barbarians* and *Burger's Daughter.*" *Ariel* 17, no. 3 (July 1986): 3–21.

Mayoux, Sophie. "J. M. Coetzee and Language: A Translator's View." *Commonwealth* 9, no. 1 (Autumn 1986): 8–10.

Memmi, Albert. *The Colonizer and the Colonized.* London: Souvenir Press, 1974.

le Past "

Moodie, T. *The Rise of Afrikanerdom*. Berkeley: Univ. of California Press, 1975.

Müller, Helene. "Who is Michael K?" *Standpunte* 38, no. 1 (February 1985): 41–43.

Musiker, Naomi. *South African History*. New York: Garland, 1984.

Ngubane, Jordan K. *An African Explains Apartheid*. New York: Praeger, 1963.

Niven, Alastair. *The Commonwealth Writer Overseas*. Bruxelles: M. Didier, 1976.

Norton, Linda. "Analysis of Michael K," unpublished paper.

O'Brien, George De. *Hegel on Reason and History*. Chicago: Univ. of Chicago Press, 1975.

Olsen, Lance Martin. "Nameless Things and Thingless Names: An Essay on Postmodern Fantasy." Ph.D. diss., Univ. of Virginia, 1985.

———. "The Presence of Absence: Coetzee's *Waiting for the Barbarians*," *Ariel* 16, no. 2 (April 1985): 44–56.

Owen, Roger. "Sunset in the West." Review of *Dusklands* by J. M. Coetzee. *Times Literary Supplement* 4163 (14 January 1983): 30.

Packer, George. "Blind Alleys." Review of *Foe* by J. M. Coetzee. *Nation* 244 (28 March 1987): 402–5.

Palmer, Eustace. *The Growth of the African Novel*. London: Heinemann, 1979.

Palmer, Eve. *The Companion Guide to South Africa*. London: Collins, 1978.

Parker, Kenneth, ed. *The South African Novel in English*. New York: Africana Publishing, 1978.

Penner, Dick. "J. M. Coetzee's *Foe*: The Muse, the Absurd, and the Colonial Dilemma." *World Literature Written in English* 27, no. 2 (Autumn 1987): 207–15.

———. "Sight, Blindness, and Double-Thought in J. M. Coetzee's *Waiting for the Barbarians*." *World Literature Written in English* 26, no. 1 (Spring 1986): 34–45.

Post, Robert M. "Oppression in the Fiction of J. M. Coetzee." *Critique* 27, no. 2 (1986): 67–77.

Rhedin, Folke. "Sydafrikansk litteratur under 70-talet." *Bonniers litterära magasin* (Stockholm) 53, no. 1 (1984): 4–13.

Rich, Paul. "Apartheid and the Decline of Civilization Idea: An Essay on Nadine Gordimer's *July's People* and J. M. Coetzee's *Waiting for the Barbarians*." *Research in African Literatures* 15, no. 3 (1984): 365–93.

———. "Tradition and Revolt in South African Fiction: The Novels of André Brink, Nadine Gordimer, and J. M. Coetzee." *Journal of Southern African Studies* 9, no. 1 (October 1982): 54–73.

Roberts, Sheila. "Character and Meaning in Four Contemporary South African Novels." *World Literature Written in English* 19 (1980): 19–36.

———. "South African Post-revolutionary Fiction." *Standpunte* 35, no. 3 (June 1982): 44–51.

"Round Table on the Works of J. M. Coetzee." *Commonwealth* 9, no.1 (Autumn 1986): 50–58.

Saul, John S. *The Crisis in South Africa*. New York: Monthly Review, 1986.

Sévry, Jean. "Variations on the Works of J. M. Coetzee." *Commonwealth* 9, no. 1 (Autumn 1986): 18–31.

Smith, Roland. "Allan Quartermain to Rosa Burger: Violence in South African Fiction." *World Literature Written in English* 22, no. 2 (1983): 171–82.

————. "The Seventies and After." In *Olive Schreiner and After: Essays on Southern African Literature in Honor of Guy Butler*, edited by Malvern Van Wyk Smith and Don Maclennan, 196–204, 233. Cape Town: David Philip, 1983.

Steinbeck, John. *The Grapes of Wrath*. New York: Viking-Bantam, 1971.

Steiner, George. "Master and Man." *New Yorker* 58 (12 July 1982): 102–3.

Strauss, Peter. "The Ending of *In the Heart of the Country*." In *Momentum: On Recent South African Writing*, edited by M. J. Daymond, et al., 121–27. Pietermaritzburg, South Africa: Univ. of Natal Press, 1984.

Sussman, Andrew. "Out of the Shadows: Books in South Africa." *Publishers Weekly* 221 (23 April 1982): 24–30.

Thiher, Allen. *Words in Reflection: Modern Language Theory and Postmodern Fiction*. Chicago: Univ. of Chicago Press, 1984.

Thompson, Leonard. *The Political Mythology of Apartheid*. New Haven: Yale Univ. Press, 1985.

Tomalin, Claire. "No Limelight for Mr. Coetzee." *Sunday Times* (London) 30 October 1983, 11.

Tutu, Desmond. *Hope and Suffering*. Grand Rapids: W. B. Eerdmans, 1984.

————. Interview with Marc Cooper and Greg Goldin. *Rolling Stone* 461 (21 November 1985): 29–30, 34, 104, 106.

————. "Mythology." Review of *The Political Mythology of Apartheid* by Leonard Thompson. *New York Review of Books* 32, no. 14 (26 September 1985): 3–4.

Uhlig, Mark A. *Apartheid in Crisis*. New York: Vintage Books, 1986.

Van Lierop, Karen. "A Mythical Interpretation of J. M. Coetzee's *Life and Times of Michael K*." *Commonwealth* 9, no. 1 (Autumn 1986): 44–49.

Vaughan, Michael. "Literature and Politics: Currents in South African Writing in the Seventies." *Journal of Southern African Studies* 9, no. 1 (1982): 118–38.

Viola, Andre. "Survival in J. M. Coetzee's Novels." *Commonwealth* 9, no. 1 (Autumn 1986): 11–17.

Wasiolek, Edward. *Dostoevksy: The Major Fiction*. Cambridge: M.I.T. Press, 1964.

Watson, Stephen. "Colonialism in the Novels of J. M. Coetzee." *Research in African Literatures* 17 (1986): 370–92.

Wautheir, Claude. "Au Coeur de la Barbarie Sud-africaine: J. M. Coetzee." *L'Afrique littéraire* 75 (1985): 90–92.

White, John J. *Mythology in the Modern Novel*. Princeton: Princeton Univ. Press, 1971.

Wilcox, A. R. *Rock Paintings of the Drakensberg*. London: Max Parrish, 1956.

Wood, W. J. B. "*Dusklands* and 'The Impregnable Stronghold of the Intellect.' " *Theoria* (1980): 13–23.

————. "*Waiting for the Barbarians*: Two Sides of Imperial Rule and Some Related Considerations." *Momentum: On Recent South African Writing*. Edited by M. J. Daymond, et al., 129–40. Pietermaritzburg, South Africa: Univ. of Natal Press, 1984.

Zille, Helen. "Police Wound Students, Arrest 25 in Protest at South Africa's U." *Chronicle of Higher Education* 33, no. 34 (6 May 1987): 44–47.

————. "South Africa Issues Stiff Rules to Check Unrest on Campuses." *Chronicle of Higher Education* 34, no. 9 (28 October 1987): 1, 45.

Index

Of Mice and Men, 95
Olsen, Lance, 23, 76

Packer, George, 129
Paine, Thomas, 8
Pascal, Blaise, 69
Pastoral tradition, 58
Paton, Alan, 16, 66, 86–87, 89
Paz, Octavio, 69
Philip, David, 15
Pirandello, Luigi, *Six Characters in Search of an Author*, 120–21
Plaasroman (farm novel), 101–2
Pope, Alexander, 46
Post, Robert, 89, 92
Power and the Glory, 38
Prix Femina Etranger, xiii, 1
Publishers Weekly, 15

Ravan Press, 15, 31, 55
Rich, Paul, xiii, 22, 58, 66, 75
Richardson, Samuel, 116, 131; *Clarissa*, 131
Roberts, Sheila, 20, 61
Robinson Crusoe, 1, 22, 113–15
Rousseau, Jean Jacques, 8, 69
Roux, Michiel le, 10–11

Sartre, Jean Paul, 69
Schreiner, Olive, 58, 100; *Story of an African Farm*, 58
Shakespeare, William, *The Tempest*, 116
Sisyphus, 115
Six Characters in Search of an Author, 120–21
Skinner, Douglas Reid, 20
Smith, Pauline, 100
Smith, Rowland, 23, 55, 61–62, 76
Smollett, Tobias, 116
Sophocles, *Oedipus Rex*, 68–69
South Africa: African National Congress and, 12; apartheid in, 9, 62–66; censorship in, 15–20, 91; colonialism and, 24–28; history of, 7–13, 47–52, 66–67; homelands policy of, 9; Immorality Act of, 9; Karoo area of, 2; Liberal Party in, 26; Mixed Marriages Act of, 9; Nationalist Party of, 9, 12, 56; oppression in, 18–20, 133–34; politics of, 16–17; Population Registration Act of, 9, 91; Publications Act of, 15–16; racial relations in, 7–13, 19–20, 58–73, 90–92, 101; Suppression of Communism Act in, 15; writers in, xiv-xv, 14–20, 58, 131–34
Steinbeck, John: *Grapes of Wrath*, 100–7; *Of Mice and Men*, 173
Steiner, George, 76
Sterne, Laurence, 94–95
Stevens, Wallace, 69
Surrealism, 57
Swift, Jonathan, 61

Tolstoi, Leo, *Anna Karenina*, 131
Tom Jones, 118–19
Trial, 91–92

Ulysses, 50
University of Cape Town, 18–19
University of Tennessee, 19
University of Texas, 2–3, 33

Van den Heever, C. M., 100
Van Riebeeck, Jan, 8
Vaughan, Michael, 22, 55, 66, 75

Waiting for the Barbarians, xiii, 1, 16, 21–23, 26, 37, 38, 46, 98–99, 132; achievement in, 75; allegorical aspects in, 75–87; colonialism in, 75–87; critical reception of, 75–76; double-thought theme in, 79–81, 86–87; dreams, 81–84; ethics in, 84–87; gender relations in, 77–84; labyrinth theme in, 81–84, 86; language in, 85; master-slave theme in, 77–87; narrative techniques in, 81–84; prose style in, 75; racial relations in, 78–84; setting of, 76, 81–82; sexuality in, 78–87; sight and blindness in, 75–79; South African aspects of, 86–87

About the Author

DICK PENNER is Professor of English at the University of Tennessee. He has written *Fiction of the Absurd, Alan Sillitoe*, and numerous articles.